# An Anthology of the Jesus-centered Deists

# Volume One: 1694 – 1730

Edited by Joseph Waligore

Socratic Spirituality Press
2025

Copyright © 2025 by Joseph Waligore

ISBN: 979-8-9920923-0-1 (Print)
ISBN: 979-8-9920923-1-8 (ebook)

Cover pictures: Matthew Tindal, John Trenchard, Anthony Collins, Thomas Gordon

Cover design and interior formatting: Michelle Stage

Published by: Socratic Spirituality Press, LLC.

The Socratic Spirituality Press is an independent press specializing in academic books that advance knowledge of the Socratic Spiritual Tradition. For more information about the Socratic Spirituality Press, go to www.SocraticSpiritualityPress.com.

# Table of Contents

Introduction to Jesus-centered Deism .................... 1

The Early Writings of Matthew Tindal .................... 4

John Toland ............................................. 22

The Early Writings of Anthony Collins ................... 35

John Trenchard and Thomas Gordon ........................ 46

The Later Writings of Anthony Collins ................... 84

James Pitt .............................................. 99

The Later Writings of Matthew Tindal ...................112

Appendix ...............................................129

# Introduction to Jesus-centered Deism

The Jesus-centered deists were very different from most people's ideas of deists. Most people see deism as the belief in a distant and inactive God who made the world but then withdrew from it. In fact, the deist God is often described as a "watchmaker" deity because, like a watchmaker, the deist God is thought to have made the universe but then left it to run on its own. Furthermore, the deists are considered to have so strongly emphasized science and rationality that they had no real religious feeling or relationship with God.

The Jesus-centered deists did not believe in a distant and inactive "watchmaker" deity who was uninvolved with the world. They believed that God loved and cared for people and had an intimate relationship with them. Many deists believed in miracles. One of the best-known Jesus-centered deists, Ben Franklin, believed that God had performed miracles to help free America from tyrannical kings during the American Revolution. Many other Jesus-centered deists believed that Jesus performed miracles, and all of the Jesus-centered deists believed that God was involved with his creation and actively cared for it. These deists also had a close relationship with God and often prayed to their loving and caring father.

While the Jesus-centered deists are very different from most people's idea of deism, they were deists because they fit the common scholarly definition of an Enlightenment deist, which was a person who believed in natural religion and used it as the rule and judge of any supernatural revelation. (Natural religion is the religion people know about solely through their natural faculties, including reason, conscience, and feelings. Natural religion does not mean a religion that denies the supernatural; it is just the religion people are aware of before or without a supernatural revelation.)

The Jesus-centered deists undermine the common idea that deism was a halfway house to atheism. This is important because many people have accepted a grand narrative of the evolution of the Western culture and of human civilization in general. In this narrative, humans at first did not understand the world scientifically, but instead saw gods, spirits, or God as behind natural phenomena. But in the 1600s and 1700s, this changed due to the rise of science and rationality. Deists are often seen as playing a major role in this cultural change because they are seen as leading advocates of science and rationality.

Because the Jesus-centered deists do not fit into this narrative about the evolution of Western culture, they have been almost totally ignored by scholars. Through research in seventeenth- and eighteenth-century books, pamphlets, and speeches, I have discovered fifty-six deists who said they were Christians and devoted their religious writings to explaining their interpretation of Christianity. Other than the three well-known American Founders, Franklin, Thomas Jefferson, and John Adams, these Jesus-centered deists are obscure figures of no importance except to scholars. But as a group, these fifty-six deists are important for our understanding of Western religious history and the evolution of Western culture. In my book, *The Spirituality of the English and American Deists: How God Became Good*, I argue that the Jesus-centered deists and most other deists were much more spiritually oriented than people think. Most deists cared deeply about God and had a close personal relationship with God. I also argue that the Jesus-centered deists and many other deists were the first major, modern Western group to be spiritual but not religious, as long as that phrase is limited to meaning people who believed in God and were outside of any traditional religious structure.

I call these deists "Jesus-centered deists," but none of them called themselves by that name. They all said they were Christians, and several labelled themselves "Christian deists." Their version of Christianity, however, was very different than how most people think of it. These deists asserted that true Christianity was only Jesus' original teachings, and they ignored or rejected any other teachings in the Bible. The Jesus-centered deists maintained that Jesus taught only that people would enter heaven after they died if they loved God and loved their neighbors as themselves. These deists asserted that Jesus' followers had added all the other Christian doctrines because these followers were either misguided or wanted to increase their power and social status. As the Jesus-centered deists' view of Christianity is so markedly different from how most people think of Christianity, it does not seem an accurate description to call them "Christian deists." However, because their religious writings were centered on Jesus' teachings, calling them "Jesus-centered deists" does seem to accurately describe them.

There are four volumes in this series of the writings of the Jesus-centered deists. The first volume deals with the pioneering Jesus-centered deists who published their writings between 1694 and 1730. The selections are grouped by author in a roughly chronological order, starting with Matthew Tindal who published the first piece by a Jesus-centered deist in 1694.

All these pioneer deists lived and worked in England, and all the biographical information about them comes from the *Dictionary of National Biography*.

In the 1600s and 1700s, many words were spelled differently than they are now. Moreover, capitalization, punctuation, italicization, and sentence length were all different than they are now. These have all been modernized to make the word-for-word excerpts more accessible to contemporary readers.

CHAPTER ONE

# The Early Writings of Matthew Tindal

Matthew Tindal, whose father was a Protestant minister, was baptized in 1657 in Bere-Ferrers, Devon. He went to Oxford University where he became a Doctor of Civil Law and was elected to a law fellowship. He converted to Roman Catholicism for a short time around 1687 but returned to Protestantism in early 1688. He was a prominent lawyer and appointed Deputy Judge-Advocate of the Fleet. In 1694, he argued a case about the rights of the sea and piracy that won him the favor of the crown. For this and other services to the crown, he was granted a yearly pension of 200 pounds. He wrote many controversial pamphlets and books about politics and religion, one of which (*A Defence of the Rights of the Christian Church*) was ordered to be burnt in 1710 by the House of Commons. His most enduring book was *Christianity as Old as Creation*, which has often been labelled "the deists' Bible." He died of a gallstone in 1733.

## *Against the Trinity*

In the 1630s and 1640s, England fought a civil war in which religion played an important part. In 1660, the side that favored the Church of England was the ultimate victor in the civil war, and the Church of England was re-established as the official national church. The leaders of this church then imprisoned thousands of Protestants who did not accept their view of Christianity. The mass imprisonments had ended by the 1690s, but people who had denied the Trinity (the belief that Jesus was God along with God the Father and the Holy Spirit) were still being imprisoned. Orthodox Christians said that belief in the Trinity was a mystery beyond people's ability to understand with their reason, but God still required belief in it. Tindal countered that it was impossible for people to believe in a mystery because they had no idea what the words meant. He further argued that God was too good to order people to believe in something that they could not understand. Instead, Tindal asserted that God told people in clear and understandable language what God wanted them to believe and practice. Tindal also said that part of Christ's mission was to abolish religious mysteries. This excerpt comes from *A Letter to the Reverend the Clergy of Both Universities, Concerning the Trinity* (n. p., 1694), 32-35.

The chief artifice by which the doctrine of the Trinity has so long prevailed is by persuading people that they must not examine into the reasonableness of it because it is a mystery, which they say is above reason and which we ought to believe whether we apprehend it or not. Children, like white paper, are capable of any impression, and if they must not, when men, examine into the reasonableness of what they have been taught [simply] because it is pretended to be a mystery, they may be obliged to assert the most absurd and senseless things as well as the most rational . . . .

As we cannot believe where we have no ideas, so we cannot believe those ideas that are contradictory to be true because they contain an affirmation and a negation of the same thing. If it were possible to believe either a mystery or a contradiction, it seems more easy to believe the latter, because in a contradiction we have ideas, and those too so clear and distinct, that we know it is impossible to predicate them at the same time of any one subject, whether divine or human. But in a mystery, we have no ideas at all. By this anyone may judge of this grand dispute between the Trinitarians and Unitarians concerning mysteries in general. And particularly the deepest of all mysteries, those of the Trinity, which the latter say they are incapable of believing because they have no ideas concerning them or none but contradictory ones. They [the Unitarians] do not disbelieve them because they cannot (as their adversaries most disingenuously object against them) apprehend the manner how they are done, but because they do not apprehend what the things are that are to be believed. On the contrary, the orthodox upon all occasions thunder it from their pulpits that matters of faith are above reason and that God has a right to require of us to believe on his word [the Bible] what we do not apprehend or understand. That is, we must believe those ideas we have of a mystery to be true, though by its being a mystery we have no ideas at all concerning it....

Whatsoever God has designed we should believe, he has made us capable of having clear and distinct ideas of. But though it should be granted that we may have false conceptions and ideas of things, yet the utmost we can do, is to believe or not believe those ideas. Where they fail, there our belief must end. God has set the same limits to our belief as to our perception. And belief belongs to us as we are rational creatures. What is above our reason to apprehend is also above our belief. Without the bounds of our reason, we are but upon the same level with beasts, and we are no more than they capable of belief or of having anything revealed to us.

As we are not capable of believing where we have no ideas, or none but contradictory, so where we have clear and distinct ideas, we cannot be mistaken without destroying the principles and foundation of all knowledge and all evidence, even of the existence of a God and of all religion, as well natural as revealed. For what other motive have I to believe there is a God, but because my reason gives me clear and distinct ideas of the truth of it? And it is by reason alone that we can judge whether

God has any revealed will, or which is his revealed will. And if there should be anything in that which is said to be his revealed will contrary to reason, it would destroy the only argument we have to believe it the word of God. Reason is as much the word, the will, and revelation of God as the written word itself, and without which the written word would be wholly useless....

To say three persons and one person are the same God is as great a contradiction as to say three persons and one person are the same. Because, as I have already proved, God and person are the same. Which instead of being a rational faith, destroys both our reason and faith. But because mystery has been the pretense by which some men for so many ages have solemnly repeated propositions as necessary to salvation, which they could no more apprehend than a round square or a mountain without a valley, I shall add one word or two more concerning it, and then conclude.

Mystery can never be a part of religion because it cannot tend to the honor of God, since it is what we know of God, not what we do not know, that makes us honor him. The more we know of him, the more we honor him. And the less there is of mystery in religion, the brighter and clearer it appears. And it would be inconsistent with the goodness of God, who would have all men come to the knowledge of his truth, not to give us clear and distinct ideas of what we are to believe or practice. His laws are a trial of (what is in our power) our obedience, but not of (what is not) our understanding. And how difficult soever they are in their practice, they are plain and easy in their theory, and suited to the capacity of the unlearned and simple, far the greatest part of mankind. As mystery can no ways tend to the honor of God, so it can no ways promote ... the good of man. Mysteries are so far from being a part of religion that it was the chief end of Christ's coming to destroy them, that is by revealing them, which is the only way a mystery or secret can be destroyed. And the end of the apostles' mission was to make known those things which until then were mysteries and to bring to light ... the hidden things of God.

In short, if Christ and Antichrist are diametrically opposite, the signs and characters that belong to each must be as opposite.

Can mystery, to which may be added persecution (the only art by which popery [Roman Catholicism] has prevailed) which are the chief signs and characters of Antichrist, and are written on the forehead of the mighty whore by pretense of which she displays her horrid blasphemies, be signs and tokens to discover Christ and his doctrine by? What has Christ to do with Antichrist? Or is the faith our Savior taught so near akin to the idolatrous blasphemies of the man of sin [the Antichrist] that both should have the same marks, the same characters, the same tokens?

## *Against the High Church Clergy*

To understand this excerpt, it is necessary to know that there were many ministers in the Church of England who brought Roman Catholic practices and ideas into the Church of England. These ministers, known as "High Church" clergy, especially emphasized how elevated the priests and bishops were above ordinary people and even emperors. Tindal collected passages from the books of various High Church leaders that emphasized this point. He also collected passages that showed how the High Church leadership took positions that deviated from fundamental Protestant positions, including the priority of the Bible and the right of every Christian to read the Bible. Tindal published these passages in *A New Catechism With Dr. Hickes's Thirty Nine Articles*, 3rd ed. (London, 1710). The following excerpt comes from pages 14-15 & 20. (In the original, Tindal gave references for these passages, but the references are not included in this excerpt.)

Q. Can the priest then forgive sins?

A. The priests have power not only to judge when we are clean, but to put away our uncleanness. As lords forgive debts of money, so they [priests] forgive debts of sin.

Q. May I be saved by the absolution of a priest?

A. Heaven itself waits the sentence from the priest's mouth, and God himself follows the judgment of his servant, the priest.

Q. Can I think too highly of this power?

A. All indifferent judges must prefer the power of obliging God to open and shut heaven's gates before a thousand kingdoms.

Q. What other power belongs to a priest?

A. Every priest is one of the principal ministers in God's kingdom, to preside in his worship, publish his laws, pass his pardons, and represent his person.

Q. What is your notion of a priest?

A. He is an advocate, mediator, intercessor, negotiator, representative, vice-regent, mandatory interpollant [intermediary] between God and man in their spiritual addresses to and negotiations one with another. He stands and acts as mediator between both parties, as it were in the middle line of conversation and in the very center of communication between them. . . .

Q. Is Christ our only advocate in heaven?

A. No, we may retain blessed advocates in heaven to plead in our defense.

Q. Who has greater power, a priest or an emperor?

A. The priesthood is a princely power, greater and more venerable than that of the empire. There is the like difference between these two powers as between little boys acting the parts of magistrates and magistrates themselves. And the spiritual government is much more excellent than the civil as heaven is than Earth, yea much more so. The priests, as if they were translated into heaven, made something above men and exempt from human affections are advanced to the princely power.

Q. You have given us a just account of the honor that's due to a priest by High Church principles. Pray let us know how a bishop is to be honored?

A. Let the bishop be honored among you as a god.

Q. Is the bishop accountable to any mortal?

A. He who makes himself judge of the bishop makes himself judge of God.

Q. How great ought the revenue of a priest to be?

A. If they administer so many things to a king who administers peace and war for bodily safety, ought they not to administer more liberally to him, who administering the priesthood towards God, secures both body and soul by his prayers?

Q. Who is guilty of the greatest treason, he who resists a king or he who resists a priest?

A. A priest no doubt. For as the priesthood is more excellent than the kingly office, so he is more worthy of greater punishment who dares move his eye against it. . . .

Q. What think you of the papists hindering the laity from reading the scripture?

A. The promiscuous license which the Protestants give to all sorts to read and interpret scripture is more prejudicial, nay pernicious, than the over-rigorous restraint of the Romanists.

Q. What is your opinion of the Inquisition?

A. Till now I never understood the reason of the policy and prudence of the Spaniards in suffering the Inquisition amongst them. And certainly it will never be well with us, till something like to the Spanish Inquisition be in England.

Q. What opinion have you of unwritten tradition?

A. Some of the ordinances observed in the church we have taught us in express words of scripture, and some we have received as delivered in secret by tradition from the apostles. Both which are of like use unto godliness. For if we attempt to lay aside the unwritten customs and usages of the church as not being of great moment, we do not know what harm we shall do the Gospel by our imprudence. In all probability, we shall thereby reduce the preaching of it to an empty name.

## *The Illegitimacy of Protestant Creeds*

Tindal argued that the Christian clergy have never been content to leave the Christian religion simple and pure as it was taught in the Bible. Instead, they want to increase their authority and power by writing creeds filled with abstruse ideas that people must believe or they will be excommunicated. He argued that the people who wrote these creeds were not inspired by the Holy Spirit, but by ordinary human passions. He said that the only way Christianity could be restored to its original simplicity was if the laity took power back from the clergy and restored the simple and plain Gospel teachings of Jesus. This excerpt comes from *The Rights of the Christian Church Asserted*, Part 1, 2nd ed. (London, 1706), 190-221.

It is absolutely necessary for the preservation of religion, in its purity and simplicity, that all the power man is capable of should belong to the laity, they can have no motive, no temptation to abuse it by corrupting religion to advance their temporal interest....

But it is the clergy's interest, on the contrary, to have it corrupted because they, as such, have no other way to gain a power of lording it over their brethren. And there is no notion so absurd but what's their interest to advance, though it seems to have no direct tendency that way. Since, when once believed, it will serve to draw on others which have. Let reason be baffled in one point, and you can never plead her sovereignty in another: *uno absurdo dato, mille sequuntur* [given one absurdity, a thousand follows]. And a rational religion will not make men depend much on the authority of the priest because [they] themselves can judge of that by its own evidence. But the more unaccountable, uncertain, obscure, perplexed, and unintelligible religion is, the more it is above their [the laity's] understanding and capacity, and the more they must pay a blind deference and submission to the dictates of the priests. And, therefore, it is no wonder if religion has been more or less confounded as they have been more or less trusted with power. And it is naturally impossible it should be otherwise. Since to be sure, some will be always attempting, though ever so much to the prejudice of religion, to introduce such opinions as are for their interest and serve to render their persons sacred and raise their character....

What a folly and madness is it to take the clergy's word in things relating to their own power and jurisdiction. And suffer them to judge in their own cause and decide where their own interest is concerned, as they must if they are judges in matters of religion. Then to be sure their own independent power shall be a fundamental article.

There never was a [Church] Council since the times of the apostolic purity that has not determined something or other in prejudice of the true religion, which was corrupted proportionally to the frequency of synods. Where no doctrine, though ever so absurd, and which men singly perhaps would have been ashamed to maintain, was not long boggled at, provided it was sufficiently adapted to their interest. Witness all the popish tenets, so very unaccountable, that the clergy, except they had been assembled in council where numbers countenance one another, and where they have the pretense of the [Holy] Spirit to sanctify whatever they do, dared not have attempted to impose them on the people....

And this opinion they confirm by the authority of Saint Gregory Nazianzus, who in his letter to Procopius, tells him, "that he fled all assemblies of bishops because he never saw a good and happy end of any council, but that they did rather increase than lessen the evil. That the love of contention and ambition always overcomes their reason." Nazianzus' judgment is the more to be regarded because it was the result of frequent trial and long experience. For he had been at several councils, particularly at the general and creed-making one of Constantinople....

If there ever was a council which acted upon other principles, there is little doubt it was the first and ecumenical one of Nice. "Which yet," as Mr. [Andrew] Marvell justly observes, "was a pitiful human business, attended with all the ill circumstances of other worldly affairs, conducted by a spirit of ambition and contention. The first, and so the greatest ecumenical blow, that by Christians was given to Christians. It was," says he, "their imposition of a new article or creed upon the Christian world, not being contained in express words of scripture, to be believed with divine faith, under spiritual and civil penalties, contrary to the privileges of religion. And their making a precedent, followed and approved by all succeeding ages, for most cruel persecutions, which only could animate men. In digging thus for a new deduction, they undermined the fabric of Christianity. To frame a particular doctrine, they departed from the general rule of their religion and violated our Savior's first institution of a church not subject to any additions in matters of faith, nor liable to compulsion."...

As to the pretense of synods being influenced by the Holy Spirit, I need only say that their conduct is a sufficient demonstration to the contrary, since those benign virtues which are the product of that [Holy] Spirit are likelier to be found anywhere else than in such assemblies. And it would be strange if divinity should choose to dwell where humanity was seldom to be found. Can the Holy Spirit be supposed to influence councils which contradict one another so much that there have been few or no questions of any moment... agitated in them which have not received opposite determinations? This is so notorious that none who is the least acquainted with church history but must with honest [Reverend William] Chillingsworth say, "I see plainly and with my own eyes that there are popes against popes, councils against councils, some fathers against others, the same fathers against themselves, a consent of the fathers of one age against the consent of the fathers of another age, the church of one age against the church of another age." Is it not the way to have a cursed church if the clergy, for instance, in one council shall curse and anathematize all who worship images, and quickly after it, in another curse all who will not worship them? How did the clergy curse themselves at the Council of Chalcedon for what they did at the Council of Ephesus? And after that, how frequently did they declare for and against the Council of Chalcedon and seldom without bitterly cursing themselves? So that the religion of the clergy of that age seems mostly to have consisted in cursing. And it is well, if it had been of that age only, since there is scarce a man in being who is not under the anathema of some canon or other.

Can the Holy Spirit be supposed to dwell with those, who, as in the case of Eutychus and Nestorius, for different terms only, set the Christian world in flames and made such a division as remains to this very day? Though, it is much, the last should be treated as a heretic after his orthodox zeal had made him say to Theodosius the Younger, "Give me, O emperor, the Earth weeded from heretics, and I, in my turn, will give you heaven. Destroy with me the heretics, and I will destroy the Persians with you." Have not councils been either imperial engines or papal machines?...

If councils had been governed by the Holy Spirit, the more they were left to themselves, the less disorder and confusion would happen amongst them....

Had synods been composed of layman, none of those corruptions which favor the priestcraft, and tend to advance the interest of the clergy and to depress that of the people, would have been brought into the church. And what deprivation is there established in any church whatsoever which does not do this, either directly or indirectly, immediately or mediately? And what other reason is there why the Church of England is so pure, then that the laity had the chief hand in reforming it?

As the clergy, though few in comparison of the laity, were the inventors, contrivers, and first broachers of corruptions, so, on the contrary, wheresoever any reformations have happened, they have been carried on by the laity in opposition to the body of the clergy. For, though perhaps, there were here and there a few so honest as to prefer the truth before their interest, yet the majority of the clergy have always been against all alterations for the better. And if a man examines the state of Christendom, he will find that the more they have in any nation abounded in number, power, and riches, the more religion has been depraved. And, on the contrary, the less power and riches they have had, and the fewer their numbers have been, the more it has been preserved pure and entire. As if to keep it so, nothing more had been required than not to allow the priests sufficient means to corrupt it.

What other reason can be assigned why religion is in some popish countries more perverted than in others, then that the number, power, and riches of the clergy are greater there? And this you will find visibly true in comparing them one with another.

And as there is a vast disproportion in these respects between the popish and Protestant clergy, so religion in the last is proportionally purer. And will not the same hold in comparing Protestant countries one with another? For can it be denied that where the power, interest, and authority of the clergy is at the lowest ebb, there is not only less of those diabolical vices, hatred, malice, animosity, persecution, etc.? And in the room [place] of these, more of the angelical virtues of love, charity, friendship, benignity, etc. But men are less immoral, lewd, vicious, debauched, and irreligious, and have more of sobriety, frugality, industry, and all other moral and social virtues?

And it is no wonder, because too many in order to advance their interest, teach men to lay so much stress on things which no ways influence a good life, to which impertinences the more regard men have, the less they attend the duties of morality. And, therefore, the great neglect of it among the heathens as well as Christians must be imputed to their priests in persuading them to place religion in rites, shows, ceremonies, and other indifferent things. Which, since men can practice without controlling their darling passions, they will be sure religiously to observe to make amends for indulging themselves in their beloved vices, especially if they are persuaded such things are expiatory of sins. And, therefore, the most superstitious nations have always been the most immoral....

Let us from the beginning of the [Protestant] Reformation ascend to that of Christianity and see how things were then managed.

Then, churches, by the laws of the empire, were incapable of possessing lands or inheritances, and the clergy, as they subsisted by the alms of the people, so they were in all other matters, as I shall fully prove hereafter, wholly dependent upon them. And then religion wonderfully flourished and increased. But, when they no longer depended on their choice or their alms, but came to be nominated by one another and to have revenues and possessions of their own, which necessarily gave them authority and power in proportion to them, then religion went to wreck, and they abounded with all manner of vices [and] men running into [religious] orders for the sake of worldly grandeur. And too many of them had no regard to religion as a divine and excellent science and of real benefit to mankind, both singly and in societies, but only as they made it a trade to enrich themselves and infatuate the vulgar.

And the reason why in some barren places of Christendom, religion, notwithstanding the ignorance of the people, was not so much depraved as in happier climates is because those countries could not support any great number of priests nor bestow any great revenues on the few they had. And, consequently, the clergy were not able (nor was it so much worth their while) to introduce or keep up corruptions here as elsewhere.

Besides, their poverty was a further security to them, by hindering them from having sufficient leisure to attend the vain and groundless, though amusing and subtle, distinctions the priests coin [make up] . . .

Had the clergy been such everywhere else, religion (which is short, plain, and easy in itself, as adapted to the capacity of the generality of mankind, the simple and unlearned) had not been rendered so obscure, perplexed and intricate, nor mixed and blended with so many profound and useless metaphysical notions, and abstruse, nice, and needless speculations. The introduction of which required a great deal of labor and pains, art and skill, and could not be contrived by plain simple men who had other callings to mind. But must be the work of those who lived at ease and were masters of their whole time, and who saw how much it was their interest to render Christianity perplexed and unintelligible, that the laity might not only admire them for their deep knowledge and religion, but likewise leave it wholly to their management as being infinitely above their poor capacities and beyond their weak apprehensions.

Which design succeeded accordingly, and these profound theologians imposed on the easy people what selfish doctrines they pleased.

And to prevent their [the laity] perceiving how grossly they were abused, on pretense of informing their understanding, they [the priests] industriously kept them in ignorance by amusing them with artificial cant and learned gibberish, made up of obscure, doubtful, and undefined words. By virtue of which they [the priests] can defend any advantageous doctrine, though ever so absurd. Since it serves them to confound, not only the ignorant and men of business with hard words, but to employ the ingenious and inquisitive in intricate disputes upon unintelligible terms and hold them perpetually entangled in an endless labyrinth of words.

## *Against Religious Persecution*

When Catholicism was England's national religion, it was common for the government to persecute people who did not espouse orthodox Catholic beliefs. When England became Protestant in the 1500s, the English government persecuted people who did not accept orthodox Protestant beliefs. It was not just Catholics who were persecuted, so too were other Protestants. In fact, in the 1660s and 1670s, thousands of Protestants who did not embrace the government-approved beliefs were imprisoned. In 1697, Tindal wrote a book-length essay arguing that it was morally wrong and counterproductive for the government to ever use persecution or force to try to compel people to believe in a certain religion. This excerpt comes from *An Essay Concerning the Power of the Magistrate, and the Rights of Mankind, in Matters of Religion*, in *Four Discourses on the Following Subjects . . . Press* (London, 1709), 130-134 & 152-155.

By religion, I understand the belief of a God and the sense and practice of those duties which result from knowledge we have of him and ourselves and the relation we stand into him and our fellow creatures. Or in short, whatever appears to us from any convincing evidence to be our duty to believe or practice. . . .

The magistrate's power extends not only to those duties which one man owes another, but even to those which man owes to God. I mean those which have an influence on human life and conduce to the welfare and support of societies, viz. [namely], the acknowledging [of] a Supreme Being who can discern men's actions and is both willing and able to punish them for neglecting those duties which are necessary for the well-being of mankind. It being impossible (as is owned by Pagans as well as Christians) that any society can subsist without some notions of religion or the acknowledging of invisible powers. Therefore, the magistrate is obliged to punish those who deny the existence of a God or [deny] that he concerns himself with human affairs. It being the belief of these things which preserves them [citizens] in peace and quiet. And more effectually obliges them to be true to their promises and oaths and to perform all their covenants and contracts, and all those other duties in which their mutual happiness consists, than all the rods and axes of the magistrate. Nor can the maintainers of atheist principles, seeing they destroy [people's] conscience by subverting all religion, have any pretense from it to challenge to themselves a toleration. And this is no greater power than one man had over another in the state of nature. For an atheist may justly be reckoned an enemy to mankind whatever state they are in and, therefore, is to be disarmed and bound to his good behavior. So far, then, it's evident that the magistrate's power extends in matters of religion. . . .

Objection: It's usually said, it is not want of charity, but the greatest [charity] that can be to hinder men by force from professing such opinions as are destructive to their souls.

Answer: But I say, first, that it's against charity for the magistrate to do a real ill to his subjects when by it he, who is as fallible as those he persecutes, is as likely to promote error as truth. . . .

Secondly, I answer that opinions merely as such are not destructive of men's souls. For God, who has made man liable to mistake, does not require an impossibility of him never to be mistaken, but that he impartially searches after religious truth and sincerely endeavors to discover it by those helps and abilities he [God] has bestowed on him to that purpose. He, therefore, who does this has the satisfaction of doing his duty as a rational creature and may be sure, though he misses truth, he shall not miss the reward of it. Since he has followed as well as he could, and no more could be his duty, the only guide God has given him to judge of truth and falsehood. . . . For it is the sincerity of the heart and the goodness of the intention which God wholly regards. And the ignorant and mistaken (if it be not their own fault) are as acceptable to him as the knowing and not mistaken, since it's he who causes the differences of men's understandings as well as circumstances. Which last makes the widow's mite [small offering to God], though very inconsiderable in itself, as acceptable as the great presents of the rich [to God]. So that two men of different religion may be both in the right way to heaven provided they do their [best] endeavor to find out the truth. For it is inconsistent with justice to give being to any creature which must necessarily make it more miserable than not to be, which must be [the case] if men are to be punished eternally for unavoidable mistakes. But God, who could have no other design in creating our immortal minds than that they should be happy, has consequently given them all (since they are all equally from him) sufficient means to make them so. So that it is strangely absurd, as well as injurious, to an infinitely perfect being to suppose he is a respecter of persons or that he has made man's eternal happiness or misery to depend on such accidents as being born in England, Rome, Turkey, China, et cetera.

Promulgation is certainly essential to a law, and, therefore, those who have no opportunity of being convinced of the truth of the Gospel shall not be accountable for not believing it. But shall be judged by the law they know and not by that they did not know. Nor shall those who believe the Gospel, if after a diligent search they are mistaken in some points, be condemned for it, because those points can't be said to be sufficiently promulgated to them. To doubt of this is to question the justice of God. Therefore, I may safely conclude that whoever does what God requires from him shall be rewarded. And that God requires no more from everyone than that he use his honest endeavor, by all means, to know and understand his [God's] will as perfectly as he can, provided when known he does his utmost to live up to it. Consequently, the greatest charity the magistrate is capable of doing is not to prejudice men in their grand choice by punishments or rewards but to leave them entirely at liberty as the most likely way to find out the truth. Or if they miss it, to make their mistakes wholly innocent.

Tindal concluded his argument against the government using persecution and force in religious matters by saying this practice was inherently counter to the Protestant Reformation. Indeed, Tindal argued that the reason the Protestant Reformation had stalled was that the Protestants too often had resorted to force. This excerpt comes from *An Essay Concerning the Power of the Magistrate, and the Rights of Mankind, in Matters of Religion*, in *Four Discourses on the Following Subjects . . . Press* (London, 1709), 220-225.

As it was persecution that advanced popery, so it was freedom and toleration that ruined it and established Protestantism, the essence of which consists in everyone's having an impartial right to judge for himself and which is the necessary consequence of it—acting according to that judgment. And, therefore, as a very worthy person says, a persecutor is nowhere at home but at Rome [residence of Catholic hierarchy]. The papists, in persecuting, act consistent with their own principles. But Protestants, whilst they persecute any, condemn themselves. The former [Catholics] pretend there are doubts and difficulties in all, even the most important points of religion, and therefore, there must be, say they, some ultimate and external judge [the Catholic Church] to appeal to by whose decisive judgment all persons must be concluded. Otherwise, [there will be] so many men [and] so many minds, and the church will be filled with controversy and confusion.

The Protestants, on the contrary, say that God has appointed no such judge. But that everyone is to judge for himself and to act according to that judgment. And, therefore, since they judged the terms of communion with the Church of Rome unlawful, they acted according to their duty in separating from it, and in forming religious assemblies of their own and endeavoring to make as many converts as they could. And that they were [as] obliged to do this when the government was against them, as well as when it was for them, in Queen Mary's days as well as Queen Elizabeth's, according to the practice of the primitive Christians who held their religious assemblies contrary to the commands of the heathen government. Grant me these principles, or by any other justify the Reformation if you can and show me then how any man, or body of men, can pretend to judge for others and by force endeavor to make them profess their sentiments. . . .

It was the Protestant priests acting most apparently and shamefully inconsistent with themselves that put a sudden stop to the Reformation, which at first, like a mighty torrent, overturned all that opposed it. And here it is that the Church of Rome insults, and says that the principles of the Protestants, by which they endeavor to justify their separation from her, are so absurd that [Protestants] themselves are obliged to act contrary to them and do the very same things they condemn in her [Catholic Church]. Thus, the persecution of the popish church has been kept in countenance by the Protestants following her example, which otherwise would have appeared so odious that all must have abhorred her for it, or else obliged her to grant that liberty which would infallibly ruin her.

As persecution was the chief cause of hindering the further spreading of the Reformation, so too that we must impute it not being more perfect and complete. For, though the first reformers deserve great commendation for what they did, yet it can't be imagined that being bred up in popish darkness and superstition, they should be able to discern, much less remove, all those corruptions which had been so long a gathering, and which [their removal] could only be the work of time or men inspired. And, therefore, it's no wonder there were so many different opinions amongst them at first. But had those who succeeded them, instead of paying a blind implicit submission to their decrees and getting them established by penal laws, taken the same liberty in examining their opinions as the reformers did their predecessors, all differences, at least of any moment, would in some time have been composed [settled]. Which became impossible by the clergy's being obliged (as they valued their subsistence) to assert such opinions, right or wrong, as were established by law. And by persecution causing such animosities and prejudices amongst the different sects that instead of examining one another's opinions sincerely and impartially, they ran daily further into ignorance, superstition, narrowness, and uncharitableness.

CHAPTER TWO

# John Toland

John Toland was born on the island of Inishowen in Ireland in 1670. He was raised a Catholic but converted to Protestantism when he was sixteen. He went to Scotland and graduated from the University of Edinburgh with an M. A. in 1690. He spent a year in Holland at Leiden University from 1692 to 1693, where he encountered unorthodox thinkers and ideas. In 1696, he published *Christianity Not Mysterious*, which was so controversial that his arrest was ordered by the Irish House of Commons. He fled to England, and over the next two decades he was intermittently supported by important patrons, such as Sir Robert Clayton (director of the Bank of England) and Robert Harley (Secretary of State). With their support, Toland wrote biographies and editions of important English political writers, such as Algernon Sidney, John Milton, and James Harrington. Toland was a major promoter of the Italian mystic Giordano Bruno and of pantheistic ideas. Toland always claimed to be a Christian, but many scholars doubt that he was sincere. He died in 1722, afflicted with kidney stones.

## *Attack on Christian Mysteries*

While Matthew Tindal had published an attack on mysteries a few years earlier, Toland's 1696 attack was much longer and much more thorough. Toland started by criticizing the very common idea of the time that there were Christian doctrines, such as the Trinity, that could not be understood by reason. Christian theologians insisted that these doctrines were mysteries that had to be accepted without trying to understand them. Toland argued, on the contrary, that any revelation must be understandable, otherwise it was not revealing anything. He thought that nothing in the Gospel was mysterious and that all parts of it could be understood by reason. The first excerpt comes from *Christianity Not Mysterious . . . Mystery* (London, 1702), 1-2, 5-6, 42-43, 46, & 170.

There is nothing that men make a greater noise about, in our time especially, than what they generally profess least of all to understand. It may be easily concluded [that] I mean the mysteries of the Christian religion. The divines [ministers], whose peculiar province it is to explain them to others, almost unanimously own their ignorance concerning them. They gravely tell us we must adore what we cannot comprehend. And yet some of them press their dubious comments upon the rest of mankind with more assurance and heat than could be tolerably justified, though we should grant them to be absolutely infallible.

The worst on it is, they are not all of a mind. If you be orthodox to those, you are a heretic to these. He that sides with a party [sect] is adjudged to hell by the rest. And if he declares for none, he receives no milder sentence from all. . . .

Others assert that we may use reason as the instrument, but not the rule, of our belief. The first contend some mysteries may be, or at least seem to be, contrary to reason, and yet be received by faith. The second, that no mystery is contrary to reason but that all are above it. Both of them from different principles agree that several doctrines of the New Testament belong no farther to the inquiries of reason than to prove them divinely revealed and that they are properly mysteries still.

On the contrary, we hold that reason is the only foundation of all certitude and that nothing revealed, whether as to its manner or existence, is more exempted from its disquisitions than the ordinary phenomena of nature. Wherefore, we likewise maintain, according to the title of this discourse, that there is nothing in the Gospel contrary to reason nor above it and that no Christian doctrine can be properly called a mystery....

Whoever reveals anything, that is, whoever tells us something we did not know before, his words must be intelligible and the matter possible. This rule holds good, let God or man be the revealer. If we count that person a fool who requires our assent to what is manifestly incredible, how dare we blasphemously attribute to the most perfect being what is an acknowledged defect in one of ourselves? As for unintelligible relations, we can no more believe them from the revelation of God than from that of man. For the conceived ideas of things are the only subjects of believing, denying, approving, and every other act of the understanding. Therefore, all matters revealed by God or man must be equally intelligible and possible. So far both revelations agree.

But in this they differ: that though the revelation of man should be thus qualified, yet he may impose upon me as to the truth of the thing. Whereas, what God is pleased to discover to me is not only clear to my reason (without which his revelation could make me no wiser) but likewise it is always true. A man, for example, acquaints me that he has found a treasure. This is plain and possible, but he may easily deceive me. God assures me that he has formed man of earth: this is not only possible to God, and to me very intelligible, but the thing is also most certain—God not being capable to deceive me, as man is. We are then to expect the same degree of perspicuity from God as from man, the more of certitude from the first than the last....

What we discoursed of reason before and revelation now, being duly weighed, all the doctrines and precepts of the New Testament (if it be indeed divine) must consequently agree with natural reason and our own ordinary ideas. This every considerate and well-disposed person will find by the careful perusal of it. And whoever undertakes this task will confess the Gospel "not to be hidden from us, nor afar off, but very nigh [near] us, in our mouths, and in our hearts." (Deut. 30: 11, 14) ...

Thus, I have endeavored to show others, what I'm fully convinced of myself: that there is no mystery in Christianity, or the most perfect religion. And that, by consequence, nothing contradictory or inconceivable, however made an article of faith, can be contained in the Gospel, if it be really the word of God.

Toland brought up three common objections orthodox Christians had to his belief that there was nothing mysterious in the Gospels. The first objection was that Christian mysteries were in fact reasonable, but that human reason had been so corrupted by original sin that it was not sound enough to understand the mysteries. Toland responded that human reason was sound. The second objection was that God had a right to command his subjects to believe things they could not understand. Toland responded that a good and just God would never make such a command. The final objection was that making people believe things that they could not understand made them humbler. Toland responded that there were already so many other things that people could not understand that they did not need another to make them humble. This excerpt comes from *Christianity Not Mysterious*, 56-7, 59, & 137-139.

There remains one objection yet, upon which some may lay a mighty stress, though it's like to do them little service. Granting, say they, the Gospel to be as reasonable as you pretend, yet corrupt and depraved reason can neither discern nor receive divine verities. Ay, but that proves not divine verities to be contrary to sound reason. But they maintain that no man's reason is sound. Wherefore, I hope so to state this question as to cut off all occasion of dispute from judicious and peaceable men. Reason, taken for the principle of discourse in us, or more particularly, for that faculty everyone has of judging his ideas according to their agreement or disagreement and so of loving what seems good unto him and hating what he thinks evil, reason, I say, in this sense is whole and entire in everyone whose organs are not accidentally indisposed. It is from it that we are accounted men; and we could neither inform others nor receive improvement ourselves any more than brutes without it. . . .

## Chapter Two

Supposing a natural impotency to reason well, we could no more be liable to commendation for not keeping the commands of God than those to whom the Gospel was never revealed for not believing in Christ. For how shall they call on him in whom they have not believed? And how shall they believe in him of whom they have not heard? Were our reasoning faculties imperfect or we not capable to employ them rightly, there could be no possibility of our understanding one another in millions of things where the stock of our ideas should prove unavoidably unequal or our capacities different. . . .

But it is affirmed that God has a right to require the assent of his creatures to what they cannot comprehend. And questionless, he may command whatever is just and reasonable, for to act tyrannically does only become the devil. But I demand to what end should God require us to believe what we cannot understand? To exercise, some say, our diligence. But this at first sight looks ridiculous: as if the plain duties of the Gospel and our necessary occupations were not sufficient to employ all our time. But how exercise our diligence? Is it possible for us to understand those mysteries at last or not? If it be, then all I contend for is gained. For I never pretended that the Gospel could be understood without due pains and application, no more than any other book. But if it be impossible after all to understand them, this is such a piece of folly and impertinence as no sober man would be guilty of: to puzzle people's heads with what they could never conceive [and] to exhort to and command the study of them. And all this is to keep them from idleness when they can scarce find leisure enough for what is on all hands granted to be intelligible.

Others say that God has enjoined the belief of mysteries to make us more humble. But how? By letting us see the small extent of our knowledge. But this extraordinary method is quite needless for experience acquaints us with that every day. And I have spent a whole chapter in the second section of this book to prove that we have not an adequate idea of all the properties and no idea of the real essence of any substance in the world. It has been a much better answer that God would thus abridge our speculations to gain us the more time for the practice of what we understand. But many cover a multitude of sins by their noise and heat on the behalf of such foolish and unprofitable speculations.

After having argued that there were no mysteries in Christianity, Toland went on to explain how Christianity came to have mysteries. He first explained that in pre-Christian times a mystery was not something that could not be understood by people, but was only something that had not yet been explained to them. He said that pre-Christian priests, to make their religion more desirable, had purposefully kept things hidden from people and that these hidden but understandable ideas were called "mysteries." Toland then stated that original Christianity had no mysteries, and mysteries only entered Christianity because of Pagan influences. This excerpt comes from *Christianity Not Mysterious*, 67-73 & 151-156.

What is meant by reason we have already largely discoursed. But to understand aright what the word "mystery" imports, we must trace the original of it as far back as the theology of the ancient Gentiles, whereof it was a considerable term.... Those nations I say, ashamed or afraid to exhibit their religion naked to the view of all indifferently, disguised it with various ceremonies, sacrifices, plays, etc., making the superstitious people believe that admirable things were adumbrated [faintly indicated] by these externals. The priests but very rarely, and then obscurely, taught in public, pretending the injunctions of their divinities to the contrary lest their secrets, forsooth, should be exposed to the profanation of the ignorant or violation of the impious. They performed the highest acts of their worship [which] consisted of ridiculous, obscene, or inhumane rites in the inmost recesses of temples or groves consecrated for that purpose. And it was inexplicable sacrilege for any to enter these but such as had a special mark and privilege, or as much as to ask questions about what passed in them. All the excluded were for that reason styled the profane, as those not in [religious] orders with us [are called] the laity.

But the cunning priests, who knew how to turn everything to their own advantage, thought fit to initiate or instruct certain persons in the meaning of their rites. They gave out that such as died uninitiated wallowed in infernal mire, whilst the purified and initiated dwelt with the gods, which as well increased their veneration for as [well as] a desire of enjoying so great a happiness. The initiated, after some years' preparation to make them value what cost so much time and patience, were devoutly sworn never to discover what they saw or heard under pain of death. Though they might discourse of them amongst themselves lest too great a constraint should tempt them to blab the secret. And so religiously they kept this oath that some of them, after their conversion to Christianity, could hardly be brought to declare what passed at their initiation. . . .

Credible authors report that the [Pagan] priest confessed to the initiated how these mystic representations were instituted at first in commemoration of some remarkable accidents or to the honor of some great persons that obliged the world by their virtues and useful inventions to pay them such acknowledgements. But let this be as it will, *myein* in their systems signified to initiate . . . and *mystery* the doctrine in which he was initiated. . . .

From what has been said, it is clear that they [the Pagans] understood by "mystery" in those days, a thing intelligible of itself, but so veiled by others that it could not be known without special revelation. I need not add that in all the Greek and Roman authors it is constantly put as a very vulgar expression for anything sacred or profane that is designedly kept secret or accidentally obscure. And this is the common acceptation of it still: for when we cannot see clearly into a business, we say it is a mystery to us and that an obscure or perplexed discourse is very mysterious. Mysteries of state, sciences, and trades run all in the same notion.

But many not denying what is so plain, yet being strongly inclined out of ignorance or passion to maintain what was first introduced by the craft or superstition of their forefathers, will have some Christian doctrines to be still mysterious in the second sense of the word, that is, inconceivable in themselves, however clearly revealed. They think a long prescription will argue it folly in any to appear against them and indeed custom has made it dangerous. But, slighting so mean considerations, if I can demonstrate that in the New Testament "mystery" is always used in the first sense of the word or that of the Gentiles, viz. [namely], for things naturally very intelligible, but so covered by figurative words or rites that reason could not discover them without special revelation, and that [if] the veil is actually taken away, then it will manifestly follow that the doctrines so revealed cannot now be properly called "mysteries." ...

He [Jesus] fully and clearly preached the purest morals. He taught that reasonable worship and those just conceptions of heaven and heavenly things. . . . So having stripped the truth of all those external types of ceremonies which made it difficult before, he rendered it easy and obvious to the meanest capacities. His disciples and followers kept to this simplicity for some considerable time, though very early diverse abuses began to get footing amongst them. The converted Jews, who continued mighty fond of their Levitical [priestly] rites and feasts, would willingly retain them and be Christians too. Thus, what at the beginning was but only tolerated in weaker brethren, became afterwards a part of Christianity itself under the pretense of apostolic prescription or tradition.

But this was nothing compared to the injury done to religion by the Gentiles. Who, as they were proselytized in greater numbers than the Jews, so the abuses they introduced were of more dangerous and universal influence. They were not a little scandalized at the plain dress of the Gospel [and] with the wonderful facility of the doctrines it contained, having been accustomed all their lives to the pompous worship and secret mysteries of deities without number. The Christians, on the other hand, were careful to remove all obstacles lying in the way of the Gentiles. They [the Christians] thought the most effectual way of gaining them [the Gentiles] over to their side was by compounding the matter, which led them to unwarrantable compliances, till at length they likewise set up for mysteries. Yet not having the least precedent for any ceremonies from the Gospel, excepting baptism and the supper [communion], they strangely disguised and transformed these by adding to them the Pagan mystic rights. They administered them with the strictest secrecy. And, to be inferior to their adversaries in no circumstance, they permitted none to assist at them, but such as were antecedently prepared or initiated. And to inspire their catechumens with most ardent desires of participation, they gave out that what was so industriously hid were tremendous and unutterable mysteries.

Thus, lest simplicity, the noblest ornament of the truth, should expose it to the contempt of unbelievers, Christianity was put upon an equal level with the mysteries of Ceres [goddess of grain] or the orgies of Bacchus [god of wine]. Foolish and mistaken care! As if the most impious superstitions could be sanctified by the name of Christ. But such is always the fruit of prudential and condescending terms of conversion in religion whereby the number and not the sincerity of professors is mainly intended.

When once the philosophers thought it their interest to turn Christians, matters grew every day worse and worse. For they not only retained the air, the genius, and sometimes the garb of their several sects, but most of their erroneous opinions too. And while they pretended to employ their philosophy in defense of Christianity, they so confounded them together that what before was plain to everyone, did now become intelligible only to the learned, who made it still less evident by their litigious disputes and vain subtleties. We must not forget that the philosophers were for making no meaner a figure among the Christians than they did formally among the heathens. But this was what they could not possibly affect without rendering everything abstruse by terms or otherwise, and so making themselves sole masters of the interpretation.

These abuses became almost incurable when the supreme magistrate [the Roman Emperor] did openly countenance [accept] the Christian religion. Multitudes then professed themselves of the emperor's persuasion, only to make their course and mend their fortunes by it or to preserve those places and performance whereof they were already possessed. These continued Pagans in their hearts. And it may be easily imagined that they carried all their old prejudices along with them into a religion which they purely embraced out of the politic considerations. And so it constantly happens when the conscience is forced and not persuaded, which was a while after the case of these heathens.

## *Toland's Radical Writings*

In his first book, *Christianity Not Mysterious*, Toland claimed to be an orthodox Christian. In later writings, he made statements that were very heterodox, questioning the status of the Gospels and stating that many biblical miracles never happened. In 1699, Toland published the pamphlet *Amyntor* in which he showed there were many more manuscripts written by early Christians about Jesus' life and teachings than just the four Gospels. Toland further stated that many of the manuscripts that were not included in the Bible were revered by early Christians and considered authentic Christian teachings. Toland argued that there was no good reason that the particular manuscripts that eventually became the Gospels were chosen over other manuscripts. Toland also ridiculed the explanation of one important ancient Christian, Irenaeus, about why there should be exactly four Gospels. The excerpt comes from *Amyntor* (London, 1699), 57-58 & 50-51.

The Council of Laodicea, which was held about three hundred and sixty years after Christ and is the first assembly wherein the canon of scripture was established, could not among so great a variety of books as were then abroad in the world certainly determine which were the true monuments of the apostles but either by a particular revelation from heaven or by crediting the testimony of their ancestors. [This testimony], which was always better preserved and conveyed by writing than by oral tradition, [was] the most uncertain rule in nature [as is] witnessed [by] the monstrous fables of papists, rabbis, Turks, and the Eastern nations in both Christians and idolaters. But of any extraordinary revelation made to this Council, we hear not a word. And for the books I defend, I have the same testimony [of their authenticity] which is usually alleged in the behalf of others.

That there should be [a] first and last [Gospel], but just the number of four, I never heard of any that went about to demonstrate, except Irenaeus, the famed successor of the apostles.

And he positively affirms that there cannot be more nor fewer than four Gospels. "For," says he, "there be four regions of this world wherein we live, with four principal winds, and the church is spread over all the Earth. But the support and foundation of the church is the Gospel and the spirit of life. Therefore, it must follow that it has four pillars, blowing incorruptibility on all sides, and giving life to men." Then, he corroborates his argument from the four cherubims and the four faces in Ezekiel's vision, to wit, of a lion, an ox, a man, and an eagle. Which is the reason, by the way, why the four evangelists are painted with these emblems in the mass book and in our Common Prayer Book. So, he concludes at last, that "they are all vain, unlearned, and impudent, who after this would assert that there were more or fewer than four Gospels."

Toland later asserted that most of the Old Testament miracles were not really miracles. He stated that these supposed miracles can be explained by natural causes. One of the most significant Old Testament miracles was that the ancient Israelites were led from Egyptian captivity to the promised land by a cloud and a pillar of fire. Toland claimed that this cloud and pillar of fire was not a supernatural miracle. It was merely the Israelites carrying a beacon of fire, which the front of the army used to signal to the rest of the army. Toland argued that during ancient times it was a very common practice for armies to use fires as this kind of a beacon. The excerpt comes from *Hodegus* in *Tetradymus* (London, 1720), 5-7 & 27.

Nothing has so much contributed to create an aversion in generous spirits against the study of the Old Testament as a persuasion taken up implicitly from their childhood that it is throughout a scene of incomprehensibles and a complete system of miracles....

Now I expect that people will presently call for examples as the only adequate proofs of this assertion. The demand is extremely reasonable, and I readily acknowledge myself obliged to answer it.... [The example] I choose at present is but circumstantial and particularly concerns the pillar of cloud and fire so frequently mentioned in the Old Testament, and scarce ever mentioned by others but as a stupendous prodigy, if not the greatest and most durable of all miracles. Wherefore, I prove in this present dissertation by reasons and matters of fact equally undeniable that it was a pillar of smoke and not a real cloud that guided the Israelites in the wilderness. And that they were not two (as by most believed) but one and the same pillar, directing their march with the cloud of its smoke by day and with the light of its fire by night. For a greater illustration of my subject, I further show there was no manner of prodigy in this affair and that fire was used to the same purposes by other oriental nations. [This fire was] not moving... of its own accord or miraculously, as it is no less needlessly than absurdly imagined, but carried in proper machines of mere human contrivance which might well be called ambulatory beacons.

    The reason of such a portable fire is this. In countries well inhabited, the route of armies, though extending ever so large in front for the convenience of forage or ways, is marked by mile stones or posts, by rivers, hills, cities, villages, castles, and other remarkable places. So that they know by their orders how far they may stretch and where again to come closer together to form one camp or body. But in vast and unpracticed deserts, without any edifices at all, without noted hills, frequent rivers, or even the ruins of ancient buildings, there is a necessity of a visible guide preceding the main body, whereby the wings [of the army] may order their march and keep within a commodious distance. So, as not to straggle or any of them be lost, and to know in an instant when the army halts or encamps. Now, there is no mute sign in the world [that] can perform this at all times, but fire alone. Since the cloud of its smoke is, as everybody knows, seen very far by day, as the light of its flame is no less conspicuous by night....

    I hope by this time, I have set in the clearest light the nature and use of the pillar of cloud and fire directing the marches and stations of the Israelites in the wilderness. In such a light, I say, that no man of good understanding or void of superstition will any longer think it a miracle. For by a common rule, agreed upon no less by divines than others, that thing ought not to be reputed a miracle which can be explained by the laws of nature or ordinary means and where a perfect account is given of all appearances.

CHAPTER THREE

# The Early Writings of Anthony Collins

Anthony Collins was born in 1676 in Isleworth, Middlesex. Collins went to Eton and then Cambridge University, but he did not graduate from Cambridge. He became a lawyer, like his father and grandfather. He married and had four children, three of whom survived. When he was in his twenties, he became a friend of John Locke and did errands for Locke, such as finding books for him. Collins was part of the establishment as he was a country squire, a justice of the peace, and the county treasurer. He was noted for was his library, which was one of the largest in England as it contained around seven thousand volumes.

While a member of the establishment, Collins was also part of the deist underground as he was a friend of Matthew Tindal, John Toland, and other unorthodox thinkers who gravitated to the Grecian Coffee House. Collins was commonly seen as a deist by his contemporaries because of what he wrote about religious topics in his many books and pamphlets. Modern scholars debate whether he thought of himself as a Christian or whether he was just claiming to be one to avoid persecution for his more irreligious beliefs. He died of the stone in 1729.

## *The Discourse of Freethinking*

In eighteenth-century England, it was illegal to criticize Christian doctrines. In 1713, Collins published *Discourse of Free-thinking*. In this book, Collins argued that people should have the right to think freely about religious matters and be free to publicly express their opinions. Collins stated this was so important in religious matters because it was the only way to find religious truth. This excerpt comes from *A Discourse of Free-thinking . . . Free-thinkers* (London, 1713), 5-6, 13-14, 32-40, 43-44, 46, & 55-56.

By freethinking, then, I mean the use of the understanding in endeavoring to find out the meaning of any proposition whatsoever, in considering the nature of the evidence for or against it, and in judging of it according to the seeming force or weakness of the evidence. . . .

If the knowledge of some truths be required of us by God, if the knowledge of others be useful to society, if the knowledge of no truth be forbidden us by God or hurtful to us, then we have a right to know or may lawfully know any truth whatsoever. And if we have a right to know any truth whatsoever, we have a right to think freely . . . because there is no other way to discover the truth. . . .

If men either neglect to think or come once to be persuaded they have no right to think freely, they cannot only obtain no perfection in the sciences, but must, if they will have any opinions, run into the grossest absurdities imaginable both in principle and practice. What absurd notions of a deity have formally prevailed not only among Pagans, but even among Christians? Who, though, they did not with the Pagans suppose God to be like an ox, or a cat, or a plant, yet some of the most ancient fathers of the church no less absurdly supposed him to be material. And many Christians in all ages supposed him to have the shape of a man, until thinking about the nature of God did establish his spirituality among men of sense in every country of Christians.

What absurd notions in religion, contrary to the most obvious notions of sense and reason, overspread the whole Christian Church for many ages? Infallibility in a single person or in a [Church] Council; the power of the priest to damn and save; the worship of images, pictures, saints, and relics; and a thousand other absurdities, as gross as ever prevailed in any Pagan nation, were opinions almost universally received and believed by Christians. And what is still more wonderful, even while they received a book [the Bible] for divine revelation point blank contrary to them all. Until the thinking of a few [the Protestant reformers], some whereof sacrificed their lives by so doing, gave a new turn to the Christian world and produced a prodigious change by establishing contrary notions [Protestantism] in some countries and by obliging those who pretended to retain the old ones to vary a little out of pure shame in the explication of their phrases and expressions....

The subjects of which men are denied the right to think by the enemies of freethinking, are of all others those of which men have not only a right to think but of which they are obliged in duty to think: viz. [namely], such as of the nature and attributes of the eternal being or God, of the truth and authority of books esteemed sacred, and of the sense and meaning of those books. Or, in one word, of religious questions.

Firstly, a right opinion in these matters is supposed by the enemies of freethinking to be absolutely necessary to men's salvation, and some errors or mistakes about them are supposed to be damnable. Now, where a right opinion is so necessary, there men have the greatest concern imaginable to think for themselves as the best means to take up with the right side of the question. For if they will not think for themselves, it remains only for them to take the opinions they have imbibed from their grandmothers, mothers, or priests, or owe to such like accident for granted. But taking that method, they can only be in the right by chance. Whereas, by thinking and examination, they have not only the mere accident of being in the right, but have the evidence of things to determine them to the side of truth. Unless it be supposed that men are such absurd animals that the most unreasonable opinion is as likely to be admitted for true, as the most reasonable when it is judged of by the reason and understanding of men. In that case, indeed, it will follow that men can be under no obligation to think of these matters. But then, it will likewise follow that they can be under no obligation to concern themselves about truth and falsehood in any opinions. For if men are so absurd as not to be able to distinguish between truth and falsehood, evidence and no evidence, what pretense is there for men having any opinions at all? Which yet none judge so necessary as the enemies of freethinking.

Secondly, if the surest and best means of arriving at truth lies in freethinking, then the whole duty of man with respect to opinions lies only in freethinking. Because he who thinks freely does his best towards being in the right, and, consequently, does all that God, who can require nothing more of any man than that he should do his best, can require of him. And should he prove mistaken in any opinions, he must be as acceptable to God as if he received none but right opinions. . . .

On the other side, the whole crime of man, with respect to opinions, must lie in his not thinking freely. He who is in the right by accident only, and does but suppose himself to be so without any thinking, is really in a dangerous state as having taken no pains and used no endeavors towards being in the right and, consequently, as having no merits. Nay, as being on the same foot with the most stupid papist [Roman Catholic] and heathen [non-Christian]. For when once men refuse or neglect to think, and take up their opinions upon trust, they do in effect declare they would have been papists or heathens had they had popish or heathen priests for their guides, or popish or heathen grandmothers to have taught them their catechisms.

Thirdly, superstition is an evil, which either by the means of education or the natural weakness of men, oppresses almost all mankind. And how terrible and evil it is well described by the ancient philosophers and poets. Tully [Cicero] says, "If you give way to superstition, it will ever haunt and plague you. If you go to a prophet or regard omens; if you sacrifice or observe the flight of birds; if you consult an astrologer or haruspex [reader of omens]; if it thunders or lightnings or any place is consumed with lightning, or such like prodigy happens, as it is necessary some such often should, all the tranquility of the mind is destroyed. And sleep itself, which seems to be an asylum and refuge from all trouble and uneasiness, does by the aid of superstition increase your troubles and fears." . . .

Now, there is no just remedy to this universal evil but freethinking. By that alone can we understand the true causes of things and by consequence the unreasonableness of all superstitious fears. "Happy is the man," says the divine Virgil, "who has discovered the causes of things and is thereby cured of all kinds of fears, even of death itself, and all the noise and din of hell." For by freethinking alone, men are capable of knowing that a perfectly good, just, wise and powerful being made and governs the world. And from this principle, they know that he can require nothing of man in any country or condition of life, but that whereof he has given them an opportunity of being convinced by evidence and reason in the place where they are, and in that condition of life to which birth or any other chance has directed them. [This means] that an honest and rational man can have no just reason to fear anything from him. Nay, on the contrary, must have so great a delight and satisfaction in believing such a being exists that he can much better be supposed to fear lest no such being should exist than to fear any harm from him. And lastly, that God, being incapable of having any addition made either to his power or happiness and wanting nothing, can require nothing of men for his own sake, but only for men's sake. And, consequently, that all actions and speculations which are of no use to mankind, as for instance, singing or dancing, or wearing of habits, or observation of days, or eating or drinking, or slaughtering of beasts, in which things the greatest part of the heathen worship consisted, or the belief of transubstantiation or consubstantiation, or of any doctrines not taught by the Church of England, either signify nothing at all with God, or else displease him, but can never render a man more acceptable to him.

By means of all this, a man may possess his soul in peace, as having an expectation of enjoying all the good things which God can bestow and no fear of any future misery or evil from his hands. And the very worst of his state can only be that he is pleasantly deceived.

Whereas superstitious men are incapable of believing in a perfectly just and good God. They make him talk to all mankind from corners and, consequently, require things of men under the penalty of misery in the next world of which they are incapable of having any convincing evidence that they are required by him. They make him, who equally beholds all the dwellers upon Earth, to have favorite nations and people without any consideration of merit. They make him put other nations under disadvantages without any demerit. And so, they are more properly to be styled demonists than theists. No wonder, therefore, if such men should be so full of fears of the wrath of God that they are sometimes tempted (with the vicious) to wish there was no God at all. A thought so unnatural and absurd that even speculative atheists would abhor it. These men have no quiet in their own minds. They rove about in search of saving truth through the dark corners of the Earth....

For suppose men take up with a religion which consists in dancing or music, or such like ceremonies, or in useless and unintelligible speculations, how can they be assured they believe and perform as they ought? What rule can such men have to know whether other ceremonies and useless and unintelligible speculations may not be required of them instead of those they perform and believe? And how can they be sure that they believe rightly any unintelligible speculations? Here is foundation laid for nothing but endless scruples, doubts, and fears. Wherefore, I conclude, that everyone out of regard to his own tranquility of mind, which must be disturbed as long as he has any seeds of superstition, is obliged to think freely on matters of religion.

Fourthly, the infinite number of pretenders in all ages to revelations from heaven, supported by miracles, containing new notions of the deity, new doctrines, new commands, new ceremonies, and new modes of worship, make thinking on the foregoing heads absolutely necessary. For how shall any man distinguish between the true messenger from heaven and the impostor, but by considering the evidence produced by the one as freely as of the other?...

Sixthly, as there can be no reasonable change of opinions among men, no quitting of any old religion, no reception of any new religion, nor believing any religion at all, but by means of freethinking, so the holy scriptures, agreeably to reason, and to the design of our blessed Savior of establishing his religion throughout the whole universe, imply everywhere and press in many places the duty of freethinking.

The design of the Gospel was, by preaching, to set all men upon freethinking that they might think themselves out of those notions of God and religion which were everywhere established by law, and receive an unknown God and an unknown religion on the evidence the apostles, or first messengers, produced to convince them. And, accordingly, the apostles required nothing to be received on their authority without an antecedent proof given of their authority. St. Paul, even in his Epistles, which are all written to men who were already Christians, offers many arguments for their confirmation in the true faith with respect to all the parts of the Christian religion. Whereby, he made them and all his readers forever judges of their force. For whoever reasons lays aside all authority and endeavors to force your assent by argument alone. St. Paul likewise went frequently into the synagogues of the Jews and reasoned with them, which was not only putting the Jews upon freethinking on matters of religion, but taking (according to the present notions of Christians) a very extraordinary step to put them upon freethinking....

Seventhly, the conduct of the priests, who are the chief pretenders to be guides to others in matters of religion, makes freethinking on the nature and attributes of the eternal being or God, on the authority of scriptures, and on the sense of scriptures, unavoidable. And to prove this, I will give you an induction [list] of several particulars of their conduct.

First, it is well known that the priests throughout the universe are endlessly divided in opinion about all these matters, and their variety of opinion is so great as not possibly to be collected together....

The popish priests contend that the text of scripture is so corrupted, precarious, and unintelligible that we are to depend on the authority of their church for the true particulars of the

Christian religion. Others [Protestants] who contend for a greater perfection in the text of scripture, differ about the inspiration of those books. Some contending that every thought and word are inspired. Some that the thoughts are inspired, and not the words. Some that those thoughts only are inspired which relate to fundamentals. And others that the books were written by honest men with great care and faithfulness without any inspiration either with respect to the thoughts or words. . . .

The priests differ about the sense and meaning of those books they receive as sacred. This is evident from the great number of sects in each religion, [which is] founded on the diversity of senses put on their several scriptures. And though the books of the Old and New Testament are the immediate dictates of God himself, and all other scriptures are the books of imposters, yet are the priests of the Christian church (like the priests of all other churches) not only divided into numberless sects on account of their different interpretations of them, but even the priests of the same sect differ endlessly in opinion about their sense and meaning.

## *An Objection to Freethinking*

A major objection that Christian commentators brought up against freethinking was that there was no reason for modern thinkers to publish their criticisms of Christian doctrines because these criticisms had already been brought up and thoroughly answered in early Christian times. Collins responded by saying that these objections had never really been discussed because the early Christians had suppressed any criticism of their doctrines. This excerpt comes from *A Letter to the Reverend Dr. Rogers . . . Same* (London, 1727), 10-13.

When you say that things [about Christianity] have been established on due consideration after having been sufficiently disputed, and every objection that persons of learning and parts could suggest [has been] heard and refuted, it is to be presumed that you do not talk at random. That, as a teacher of truth, you would not invent falsehoods or say anything after others to throw dust in your readers' eyes. And that, as a learned man, you would not assert a fact of this kind which you could not prove. You will, therefore, be pleased to let us know the names of those books wherein all these matters have been sufficiently disputed and wherein every objection that persons of learning and parts could suggest has been heard and refuted. And give us an account of the discussion these things have undergone that we may see with what truth you say they were established on due consideration. For my part, I know of no such books, nor discussion, which preceded the establishment of Christianity or religion in any country. . . . And, as to the books written before Christianity became completely established in the Roman Empire, it does not appear that the Jews, who of all adversaries should seem best to understand the Christian religion and consequently best qualified to make pertinent objections, wrote any books against it. The Pagans, indeed, wrote several books against Christianity after it had been sometime in the world, but these seem to have been rather satirical than argumentative. Of which, the remains of Celsus's book preserved by Origen and of Julian's book preserved by Cyril are approved. Wherein, those two persons of great learning and parts condescend to attack Christianity by sarcasm and calumnies [slanders] and make objections which argue very little knowledge of the Jewish and Christian religions, and of the books of the Old and New Testament, and of the pretenses of Christians, whom they despised as fanatics and enthusiasts. It is said, indeed, that Porphyry's *Book against Christianity* (which is lost, as well as Eusebius's famous answer to it) was an elaborate and acute performance. Yet, I think the presumption is that it consisted, like other books and discourses against Christianity, very much of lies, satire, and declamation [pompous speech] and very little argumentation or criticism founded on a knowledge of the Old and New Testament and on a consideration of the historical facts reported by Jesus and his apostles. But however that be, it does not seem that even the objections of Celsus, Julian, and Porphyry had fair play or were refuted in the manner you suppose, much less objections of all kinds, as you assert. For by the decrees of [early Christian] Councils and edicts of the first Christian emperors, the books of the Pagans against Christianity, and the books of heretical Christians, and of the Jews were forbidden to be transcribed, or published, or read, or kept under the severest penalties and ordered to be all burnt. Which conduct prevented a due consideration of objections at first and ended in a total suppression and loss of all books written by the Pagans against Christianity and of many other books from whence information or objection in relation to Christianity could be had.

## A Defense of Ridicule

Because governmental authorities did not allow people to freely express their objections to Christian doctrines, some deists resorted to satire and ridicule to get around these restrictions. While Christian authorities often disparaged this practice, Collins defended it as necessary. This excerpt comes from *A Discourse Concerning Ridicule and Irony . . . Marshall* (London, 1729), 7 & 19-22.

And this [the satirist's] manner of writing is seldom complained of as unfit to be allowed by any but those who feel themselves hurt by it. For the solemn and grave can bear a solemn and grave attack [as] that gives them a sort of credit in the world and makes them appear considerable to themselves as worthy of a ferocious regard. But contempt is what they, who commonly are the most contemptible and worthless of men, cannot bear nor withstand as setting them in their true light. And being the most effectual method to drive imposture, the sole foundation of their credit, out of the world. . . .

In fine [summation], books of satire, wit, humor, ridicule, drollery, and irony are the most read and applauded of all books in all ages, languages, and countries. And as those which are exquisite in their kinds are the standing entertainment of the ingenious and learned, so others, of a lower kind, are to be found among the lower readers, who sleep under all works which do not make them merry.

In a word, the opinions and practices of men in all matters, and especially in matters of religion, are generally so absurd and ridiculous that it is impossible for them not to be the subjects of ridicule.

For what else can be expected from men who generally take up their opinions without any inquiry into their reasonableness or truth and upon the most incompetent grounds?...

And if some men will fall into absurd and ridiculous opinions, habits, forms, figures, and grimaces, there will be those who will laugh, nay, cannot help laughing at them. Hence, most parties [sects] laugh at one another without the least scruple and with [the] great applause of their own parties....

Laughing, therefore, and ridicule in serious matters go round the world with no inconsiderable applause and seem highly proper for this world of nonsense and folly. To hinder laughing upon such just occasions... is almost all one as to hinder breathing....

For decency and propriety will stand the test of ridicule and triumph over all the false pretenses to wit. And indecency and impropriety will sink under the trial of ridicule as being capable of being baffled by reason and justly ridiculed. And if any kind of degree of ridicule be absurd or ridiculous, that will appear so upon trial, no less than the low and gross ridicule prevalent among the unpolite part of the world. But that will never appear. On the contrary, ridicule of certain kinds and under reasonable directions and rules, and used in proper time, place, and manner (all which also are only to be found out and fixed by trial and experience), is both a proper and necessary method of discourse in many cases. And especially in the case of gravity when that is attended with hypocrisy or imposture, or with ignorance, or with sourness of temper and persecution. All which ought to draw after them the ridicule and contempt of society, which has no other effectual remedy against such methods of imposition.

CHAPTER FOUR

# John Trenchard and Thomas Gordon

John Trenchard was born in 1668/9 to an ancient family who owned significant pieces of land in western England. He graduated from Trinity College, Dublin and was a lawyer for a short while. An inheritance from both an uncle and his father meant he did not have to support himself. His first two wives died, and he married his third wife in 1719. He devoted his time and money to writing about political and religious topics. Together with Thomas Gordon, he wrote political and religious essays in newspapers using the titles *Independent Whig* and *Cato's Letters*. These essays were extremely popular when they were first published. They were also very influential throughout the eighteenth century in Britain, America, and on the European continent. Trenchard died of a kidney ailment in 1723.

Not much is known about Thomas Gordon's early life besides that he was born in Kirkcudbright, Scotland around 1696. He became a lawyer in 1716 and went to London as a young man where he made his living tutoring languages. He wrote several very well-received essays and pamphlets. His writings impressed Trenchard, who became his patron and collaborator. After Trenchard's death in 1723, Gordon was appointed first commissioner of wine licenses, a post he held until his death. In 1724, he married Trenchard's widow. He was a classical scholar and published very well-received editions of the Roman historians Tacitus and Sallust. He died in 1750 of unknown causes.

These excerpts, except for the last one, all come from the *Independent Whig*, 7th ed., 4 vols. (London, 1743). This edition is posted online at https://oll.libertyfund.org/titles/trenchard-the-independent-whig-vol-1-7th-ed-1743.

## *Clerical Corruption*

It was a common claim of Martin Luther and the other early Protestant reformers that the Catholic priests had abandoned true Christianity because the priests were corrupt people who wanted power and dominion over the laity. Gordon stated that this tendency was not limited to the Catholic priests but shared by all clergy. Gordon praised virtuous Christian ministers, but he thought corrupt clergy had brought "infinite evils" upon mankind. He said that Jesus and his first disciples were tolerant and charitable people, but later Christian clergy had perverted Christianity so that they could acquire more power and status. This excerpt comes from the *Independent Whig*, number II, entitled, "Of the Design of this Paper." In the 1743 edition, it is in vol. 1, pages 10-15.

That profession must be always most honorable and deserving from mankind, which is most useful and advantageous to men. As it is, therefore, impossible to show too much respect to virtuous clergymen, so the corrupt part of them cannot be too much exposed. Since the possession which they have of the fears and panic of superstitious people and in the tenderest seasons too enables them to do the greatest mischief, the strongest antidotes ought to be applied to their poison. It will be ridiculous to call for protection from that character which they constantly disgrace and to ask assistance from the religion which they neither believe nor practice.

I here list myself under the banners of the former sort. And design by this work to illustrate the beauty of Christianity by exposing the deformity of priestcraft. To distinguish the good clergy from the bad by giving to each his share of praise or infamy according to the different deeds done by them. I will lose no opportunity of doing justice to the former, nor willingly [to do justice] to the latter.

In doing this, I shall go far backward, and, taking things from the beginning, show in the course of these papers the infinite evils brought upon mankind from age to age by the pride and imposture of corrupt ecclesiastics. I shall show what a Babel they have built upon the foundation of Christ and his apostles, who were made to father doctrines which they never taught and to countenance power which they always disclaimed. I shall show by what arts and intrigues they came from being almsmen of the people to be masters of mankind. And how, by pretending to dispose of the other world, they actually usurped and ruled this.

I shall show that notwithstanding Christianity was first propagated by miracles and mildness only, and the teachers of it had no power but to persuade, making it withal appear in the whole course of their lives and preaching that they sought no manner of personal advantage or any manner of jurisdiction over their hearers and converts. Yet they who, without their [the apostles'] inspiration and manners, called themselves their successors did by virtue of their names lay insolent claim to dominion and carried all things before them by the dint of terror and excommunication.

I shall show that though the clergy, like other militia, were raised and paid for protecting mankind from their spiritual enemy, yet they soon made use of the sword put into their hands against their masters and set up for themselves. I shall show that, notwithstanding the whole end of their institution was to make men wiser and better, yet wherever they prevailed, debauchery and ignorance also prevailed. And the constant lesson they taught was blind belief and blind obedience, of both which they made themselves the objects. So that superstition was an inseparable creature of their power and the perpetual issue of it. And tainted morals and darkened minds were the great props of their dominion. A good understanding and an inquisitive spirit led directly to heresy. A pious life was of ill example and a reproach to the clergy. And if anyone gave offence this way, it was but calling him heretic and delivering him over to Satan, the man was then undone and the clergy safe.

I shall show how they soon banished the meek spirit of the Christian religion and growing to as great variance with mercy as they were with reason, perverted religion into rage and zeal into cruelty. They made the peaceable doctrine of Jesus a doctrine of blood, and excommunicated and damned by that name by which alone men could be saved. It is true they damned one another as much as they did the rest of the world. For agreeing in nothing but the great principle of [personal] interest, though they rode upon the necks of their people, yet they never could be at peace nor ease among themselves so long as each individual was not in the highest place. And, therefore, because every one of them could not be above all the rest, they were eternally quarrelling and giving one another to the devil.

In another essay on the topic of the corruption of the clergy, Trenchard stated that the Protestant clergy wanted as much power and dominion over people as the Catholic clergy. He also said that the Protestant clergy made sure that the Protestant Reformation in England was not a complete reformation because the Protestant clergy wanted to keep all the prerogatives of the Catholic clergy. This excerpt comes from the *Independent Whig*, number XII, entitled, "The Enmity of the High Clergy to the Reformation, and Their Arts to Defeat the End of It." In the 1743 edition, it is vol. 1, pages 92-98.

The [Protestant] Reformation in England was carried on, not only without, but against the consent of the whole body of the clergy (very few excepted), who always opposed every step towards their own amendment. It was, indeed, everywhere properly speaking, an effort or insurrection of the laity against the pride and oppression of the priests, who had cheated them of their estates, imposed upon their consciences, debauched their wives, and were ever insulting [their] persons.

The poor, injured people had long felt the malady, but were so intimidated by their own superstition and the overgrown power of their haughty masters, that they dared not think of a remedy, till a bold and disobliging friar or two dissolved the enchantment. And then, the whole Christian world seemed to rise at once against this fairy and fantastical empire [of Catholicism].

But people long used to servitude, knowing not what freedom is, or how to preserve it when thrown into their laps, have always recourse to some leaders of whose honesty and greater wisdom they have conceived a [good] opinion. And these [leaders] for the most part abuse such confidence to advance their own views of wealth and power.

So it happened in this case. And, consequently, the Reformation went partially on according to the direction under which it fell. Where priests were at the head of it, they attempted only to make it a Reformation of sounds and distinctions. They took no offence at the riches and grandeur of the clergy (which was the source of all other evils) but were angry that they had not their share of them. And so looked upon the revolt only as a means to aggrandize themselves. They condemned not the tyranny, but the tyrants. And attempted to usurp that power in their own persons which they loudly exclaimed against in the Romish [Catholic] priesthood. Most [Protestant] sects of them wonderfully well agreed that there was a divine right in the clergy to dictate to the laity in religious matters. But every sect claimed that power to themselves, independent of all others.

They [the Protestant clergy] could not agree about sharing the prey, but each would have had the whole. Which had this good effect, however, that they were all obliged to abate much of their pretensions in order to engage customers. And, I thank God, they have not yet been able to raise the price again to the old market. Though, to do them justice, they are no ways answerable to their successors for having let slip any opportunity to that purpose.

But whilst they were thus carrying on their project for dominion, they found it necessary to throw out a barrel to the whale and keep the people's minds busied and their passions afloat with metaphysical subtleties and distinctions of no use to true religion and morality, though very conducive to their own ambitious tyrannical designs.

I would gladly know from these reverend venders of trifles whether it would have been worth the thousandth part of the combustion which has been made or the blood which has been spilt only to have settled a few speculations, if they could have been settled? Pray where is the essential difference between transubstantiation, consubstantiation, and the real presence? What [is] the consequence whether a child be baptized by one sort of priest or by another? Or of what use to mankind are the abstruse questions about predestination, free will, or free grace? What is the difference, as to the duties or ordinances of Christianity, if they be administered under the direction of a single person, a bench of bishops, or a Lower House of Convocation, or none of them all, so they be piously administered? Or whether the chimerical line of [apostolical] succession be broken or ever had a being?

Since it is agreed amongst all our present sects of Christians that the Savior of the world is the Son of God descended from heaven to teach virtue and goodness to men and to die for our redemption, how are we concerned in the scholastic notions of the Trinity? Will the scripture be more regarded or the precepts of it be better observed if the three persons are believed to be three divine, distinct spirits and minds who are so many real subsisting persons? Whether the Son and Holy Ghost are omnipotent of themselves or are subordinate and dependent on the Father? Or, if they are independent, whether their union consist in a mutual consciousness of one another's thoughts and designs or in anything else? Whether they are three attributes of God, viz. [namely], goodness, wisdom and power? Or three internal acts, viz., creation, redemption and sanctification? Or two internal acts of the one subsisting person of the Father. That is to say, the Father understanding and willing himself and his own perfections? Or three internal relations, namely, the divine substance and Godhead considered as unbegotten, begotten, and proceeding? Or three names of God ascribed to him in holy scripture, as he is father of all things, as he did inhabit in an extraordinary manner in the man Jesus Christ, and as he affected everything by his spirit, or his energy and power? Or, lastly, whether the three persons are only three beings, but what sort of beings we neither know nor ought to pretend to know? Which I take to be the Trinity of the mob as well as of some other wiser heads.

As far as I can remember, these are the important questions which have set mankind together by the ears for so many ages. And it seems are yet thought of consequence enough to create new feuds and mortal dudgeon amongst all our sects of ecclesiastics. But why must we of the laity quarrel about them too? What have beaus and belles, old women, cobblers, and milkmaids to do with homoousios, consubstantiality, personality, hypostatical union, infinite satisfaction, etc.? None of which hard words, or any like them, are to be found in scripture. And therefore, I think, we may even return them to Rome [the residence of the Catholic hierarchy], that being the place from whence they came, and be contented to be good Christians without them.

We ought to show our faith and obedience to God by a cheerful submission to his commands and not affect a vain curiosity of prying into his secrets [or] pretend to philosophize upon his abstracted nature and essence. And, with our limited and corrupt understandings, assume to comprehend infinite wisdom and power and define the modus of its existence and operations. Almighty God would not make himself farther known even to Moses, nor suffer himself to be otherwise described to the children of Israel... than by the comprehensive words, "I am that I am." Which methinks might baffle our officious impertinence and put us in mind of the danger of peeping into the Ark [of the Covenant].

The above disputes make us neither wiser nor better. Men are not intended for speculation; exceeding few are capable of it. The faculties of our minds as well as the frame of our bodies are adapted to labor and to supply the exigencies of our nature. We are formed for society and mutual help, and the goodness of God has implanted in us qualities suited to these ends. He has, besides, given us precepts for our assistance and annexed infinite rewards to the observance of them. We know how to be good parents, good children, good neighbors, and good subjects. But how small a part of mankind understands or are capable of understanding metaphysical questions! When they use the terms, it is plain that they have no ideas annexed to them, but fight at blind man's bluff and quarrel about what none of them understand. It is evident, therefore, that the all-wise providence could not intend to perplex and confound weak minds with such subtleties for the knowledge of which he has not given them suitable qualifications.

## *Against Religious Ceremonies*

Gordon so hated the use of ceremonies in religion that he wrote two essays attacking them. In one essay, he said that Pagan priests had invented religious ceremonies and thus "polluted or abolished all religion." According to Gordon, while Jesus had instituted a religion without ceremonies and priests, the Catholic hierarchy had substituted Pagan ceremonies for Christianity, and therefore "holiness of heart was changed into holiness of posture." Gordon maintained that the lay people gladly accepted this change because, under the rule of Catholic priests, the laity had lost the concept of "the spiritual nature of the Gospel." This excerpt comes from the *Independent Whig*, number XXXII, entitled, "Of Ceremonies. Part 2." In the 1743 edition, it is vol. 1, pages 274-277.

Had not Pagan ceremonies (and Pagans were the first inventors of ceremonies) signified nothing or rather something very bad, as, indeed, it was evident to every eye that they were either senseless or impious, our Savior would never have instituted, as he did, a religion without one ceremony in it. The religion of the Gospel is as pure from fancies and ceremonies as from pride and the spirit of dominion.

Our blessed Savior knew well that the crafty and profane priests had by their shameless inventions and filthy ceremonies polluted or abolished all religion. And, therefore, in mercy to mankind, founded a religion without priests and without ceremonies (as shall be fully shown hereafter). For it is to be observed that while the established church of Paganism flourished, priests and ceremonies always flourished or increased together.

Such was the simple institution of the Gospel. But when popery began to expel Christianity, ignorance and ceremonies were some of the principal engines by which it effected the same. For as the meekness of Christians was then converted into the cruelty of barbarians, and the plainness of the Gospel into all the detestable fopperies of Paganism, so holiness of heart was changed into holiness of posture; the humility of the soul into bodily bowings; the worship of God into the worship of bread and the piping of organs. And the clergy, as they had called themselves, were no longer clothed with meekness, but with surplices, etc.

Nor was this mighty revolution, this unnatural transition from the beauty and gentleness of Christianity to the unhallowed spirit and abominable rituals of the heathens, at all hard or impracticable. The people had, by the idleness, insufficiency, and debaucheries of the ecclesiastics, become corrupt and blind to the last degree, and therefore ran readily and cheerfully into every new absurdity. Whatever the bishop pronounced decent, though ever so vile or silly, his conforming flock received as reverend and edifying. A gross and sensual manner of worship suited best with the grossness of their understandings and the sensuality of their minds. They had no conception of the spiritual nature of the Gospel and of that evangelical grace which operates internally and is wholly employed about the soul, but produces neither cringes nor dances, nor grimaces.

A religion therefore of ceremonies, which is no religion at all, agreed well with those carnal Christians who were taught to place all religion in ceremonies. When the ignorant vulgar are once persuaded that ceremonies are good for anything, they come quickly to think them good for everything and the more the merrier! They are delighted with shadows, and mystery, and juggling [deception]. Ignorance, like every other habit, is daily improving itself and increases in strength as in years. It delights to be still plunging into farther and deeper darkness. The less people understand, the more they stare. And because there is nothing in the Gospel but plain piety, plain reason, and plain matter of fact, therefore, it can raise no wonderment in them and consequently no pleasing piety. But strange and mysterious ceremonies can do all this, and for that reason have always got the better of religion in all bigoted countries.

In another essay on ceremonies, Gordon drove home the point about how ceremonies destroy religion. He argued that God sent Jesus to abolish all the Jewish ceremonies and that Jesus set up a religion with no ceremonies at all. However, the priests introduced ceremonies for their own purposes. Gordon asserted that where ceremonies abound in religion "there religion is either utterly lost or miserably decayed." He said that ceremonies were first introduced into Christianity for the purpose of promoting religion, but centuries of experience have shown that ceremonies become the rival and enemy of true religion. This excerpt comes from the *Independent Whig*, number XXXI, entitled, "Of Ceremonies." In the 1743 edition, it is in vol. 1, pages 262-267.

Plainness and simplicity are not more inseparable marks of truth than they are of true religion, which wants neither paint nor pageantry to recommend itself to the hearts of men. It wins the affections by the force of its persuasions and the understanding by the reasonableness of its precepts. It abhors violence as opposite to its nature and despises art and policy as below its dignity. Human ornaments may hide and disfigure but cannot preserve nor improve its intrinsic beauty and divine luster. And pomp and grimace, as they are nowise akin to it, so neither are they the effects of it nor bring any advantage to it. On the contrary, they tend to fill the mind with gross ideas or sullen fear and so create superstition instead of piety and farce instead of worship.

God himself has told us that he will be worshipped in spirit and in truth, which shows that love and sincerity constitute devotion and that religion resides in the mind. As to bodily religion and corporeal holiness, the Gospel is silent about them, leaving everyone at full liberty to behave his own way in the practice of piety.

It is justly esteemed the glory and felicity of the Christian religion that, by it, we are released from that grievous yoke and bondage of ceremonies, which neither we nor our fathers were able to bear. It is a religion of reason void of all superfluities and trifling impertinences.

Men cannot judge of one another's thoughts and inclinations but by words and actions. And, because it would be both troublesome and silly to be on every occasion haranguing our friends and superiors upon the profound veneration which we profess for their persons or characters, it has become necessary to agree upon some outward forms to denote internal respect. And this I take to be the only good reason which can be given for such manner of address or ceremony. It is ridiculous, either by sounds or gestures, to tell a man over and over again what he knows already, and therefore, the most intimate friends and old acquaintance make but little use of show or compliment. And those who make most are ever found the least sincere. But how senseless and absurd must it be to entertain heaven with such grimaces! That heaven, which searches our hearts, and knows our most hidden thoughts, and will not be deceived by outward, arbitrary, and fallacious marks of inward disposition!

It can never be conceived that the all-merciful and omniscient God should, by the sending of his son, abolish or suffer to be abolished, the whole Jewish legion of ceremonies, though appointed by himself in person, and should graciously condescend to establish a new dispensation, destitute of all ceremony and exterior grandeur, and yet should leave it to the ambition of designing men or to the folly of weak ones to invent and impose a fresh load of rituals in opposition to the plain genius of the Gospel. This would be for the all-merciful to be merciful in vain; for the creator to resign his power to the creature; and for God to recall his own injunctions, which he once gave for a gracious and wise end, since ceased, that men may enforce theirs for a weak or a wicked one.

Nothing is or can be pure religion but either what God commands and tells us he will accept or what is dictated by eternal reason, which is the law of nature. And whatever is superadded, however dignified by a venerable name, is no part of true religion, which, as has been said, can be supported by nothing but divine revelation or divine reason. When both these are wanting, we wander in the dark and worship blindfold, being led by the hand of conjecture and invention, which are uncertain and endless.

This is so true that wherever there is true religion, there are few ceremonies. And, on the other hand, where ceremonies abound, there religion is either utterly lost or miserably decayed. And, in popish countries, it [religion] is more or less visible according as ceremonies and bigotry, which, like cause and effect go always hand in hand, are more or less practiced or promoted. Thus, in France, where through the commerce of that kingdom with Protestants there are still some remains of common sense and consequently of religion, God almighty is worshipped as well as dead men, though not so much. Whereas, in Italy and Spain, the saints have deprived their maker of all devotion, and the Blessed Virgin, St. Dominic, St. Jago, and St. Antony are by these hotheaded bigots made governors of heaven and Earth and the givers of eternal life. And consequently are become, next immediately after the priests, the only objects of their adoration. If you deprive them of their saints and their ceremonies, there is not the least face of religion left amongst them.

So little has Christianity gained by ceremonies that a great part of mankind have, by adopting them, banished all true religion. If they were introduced, as it is alleged, to kindle piety, I am sorry to say it has so happened that this heat of devotion has quite drank up the truth and vitals of religion, and the blind compliance with a senseless cringe, invented and enjoined by a popish priest, is made of more importance and merit than the possession of all moral and Christian virtues without it. Religion, good sense, and humanity are inseparable friends, but a superstitious fondness for ceremonies is a contradiction and an affront to all the three.

The teachers of mankind have, for the greatest part, been the most unteachable of all men. And these, our guides to peace, have been always the foremost to break it. They have seen, from time to time, the violence and ungodly effects produced by their contention for human forms, habits, and decisions. And yet, where the religious laity and the law did not interpose to restrain this unchristian behavior in churchmen, they have not only still adhered with obstinacy to their inventions and impositions, but frequently made it their business to broach new ones and to throw about fresh balls of strife and cruelty.

Ceremonies were first brought in under a very plausible pretense: namely, that of aiding and promoting religion. But we have seen by above a thousand years' experience that these its pretended friends always become its real rivals and successful enemies. And, by the help of those whose interest it was to contrive and support them, at any rate never failed to banish it [religion] as far away as their power extended.

## *The Clearness of Scripture*

Gordon asserted that in God's first revelation to people in ancient Israel, God was extremely clear and exact about all the details of how he wanted rituals to be observed. However, in God's second revelation, which was recorded in the New Testament, many speculative things were left very vague and only the parts about how we should live were clear. Gordon stated that people make a mistake if they try to understand these obscure parts. The first part of this excerpt comes from the *Independent Whig*, essay number IX, entitled, "Of the Clearness of Scripture." In the 1743 edition, it is vol. 1, pages 63-65 & 67-71. The second part of this excerpt comes from the *Independent Whig*, number IV, entitled, "Of the Explication of the Scripture." In the 1743 edition, it is in vol. 1, pages 23-27.

I shall in this paper endeavor to confirm what I have said in my last, by showing that God almighty, in revealing his will to mankind, has always taken effectual care that it could not be mistaken. And, therefore, made it so plain as to need no further explanation in all things which are necessary for us to know.

When God would have his pleasure known to men, it is agreeable to his goodness to make it evident. When he would not, it is agreeable to his wisdom to make it impenetrable.

Scripture was not given to make work for interpreters. Nor to teach men how to doubt, but how to live. The Holy Spirit has made undeniably clear and manifest all those precepts that enjoin faith and obedience, which are the great points of religion. And weak men cannot correct him and do it better themselves.

I think it is generally granted that revelations are no more and that prophecy has ceased. The reason given for this I take to be a very good one: namely that God has already sufficiently discovered his mind to men and made his meaning manifest. If it were otherwise, we should, doubtless, have his extraordinary presence still. But as we have not, it is to be presumed that we have no occasion. He appeared himself whilst men were in darkness. But now that he has shown them his marvelous light, he appears no more. His presence is supplied by his word [the Bible], which being addressed to all men equally and not to one tribe of men to interpret it for the rest, it follows that all men have in their power the means to understand it. Old revelation, therefore, does not want the assistance of new, nor has the omnipotent any need of prolocutors [spokespersons].

While God is delivering his law to the world, he is plain even to exactness and his orders are full and circumstantial even about the minutest points. This is eminently proved by his manner of giving laws to the Jews. Every ceremony, every instrument and garment used in their worship is precisely described and directed. The trumpets, the candlesticks, the lamps, the spoons, the snuffers are all of his own appointment, both as to the materials and the use of them. He makes it impossible to mistake him....

The Decalogue, or the law of the Ten Commandments, delivered by God himself from Mount Sinai with great glory and astonishing circumstances, was little else but the law of nature reduced into tables and expressed in words of God's own choosing. And they were worthy of the omnipotent and infallible author. For they were so plain and indisputable that not a single person of all the twelve tribes [of Israel], so addicted on other occasions to contradiction and wrangling, so much as pretended not to understand them. Nor was there one man, much less a body of men, set apart to explain them.

When God spoke to the Jews by his prophets, the same method of clearness was observed. The admonitions given and the judgments denounced were adapted to the capacity of everyone concerned. The Jews, it is true, did not often believe them, at least not mind them. But it was never pleaded that they did not comprehend them. God inspired, the prophets spoke, and all understood. But neither creeds nor paraphrases were made, for they were not necessary. . . .

The Gospel, when it came, as it was to excel all other laws in its end and usefulness, so was it the shortest and plainest institution in the world. It only added the duty of faith to that of good works, which was the great, if not the only, business of the moral law. To believe that Jesus Christ was the only Son of God was the great principle of the Christian religion. Nor was the practice of this belief attended with the least difficulty, since our Savior proved his mission and omnipotence by miracles that were undeniable and convincing. For the truth of them he appealed to men's senses. There was neither mystery nor juggling [deception] in his actions, nor did they want anybody to explain them.

All this is further confirmed by the conduct of the apostles. The constant drift and tenor of their lives and preaching was to persuade mankind to believe in Jesus Christ. In order to which they worked miracles and gave the Holy Ghost. The precept was thus short and the motives to comply with it were thus irresistible. Hence, it was that sometimes thousands were convinced in a moment, without either commentaries, or creeds, or catechisms. And, indeed, who could avoid believing a proposition that proved itself?

The apostles, when they had converted one city, did not stay to establish a hierarchy there only, and to tell the same thing over and over again to those that knew it already. No, when they had planted the faith in one place, they travelled to another and preached the Gospel to the unconverted world, leaving those already converted to perform Christian worship their own way. If they believed in Christ and lived soberly, the apostles desired no more. Those were the two things needful. Nor were they more needful than clear.

In this plain manner did God almighty always discovers himself in his will whenever he dispensed his laws to men....

Upon the whole, when almighty God reveals his will, he does it effectually. But when he disguises it in dark and doubtful expressions, it is plain that the time of making himself further known to men is not yet come, and it is in vain for them to pry into his secrets.

The all-merciful being does never require of us that which we cannot find he requires. It is not consistent with his wisdom and goodness to make that necessary which he has not made plain. He has with the greatest perspicuity described the candlesticks, tongs, and other tools of worship under the Jewish law. And yet, in the Gospel has not said one word of some doctrines which we are told are necessary to salvation. Altars and priests are divinely appointed in the old dispensation but are neither directed nor described in the new. And yet, we know of what importance they are present in the popish church and elsewhere. The priest's office is particularized and circumscribed, even to the killing of a goat or a pair of pigeons. And yet, under the Gospel it is not so much as hinted that a priest shall administer either of the sacraments. Though, if we will take their own words for it, there can be no sacrament without them....

To fear God and keep his commandments is the summary of the Old Testament. And to believe that Jesus Christ is come in the flesh is the compendium of the New. Whoever can prove his obedience and faith by these two plain duties fulfils the [Old Testament] law and the Gospel.

It was most agreeable to the infinite goodness and tender mercies of God to make everything which he requires of us weak men obvious and clear. The importance of the duty implies its certainty, which is not to be found in phrases either doubtful or obscure. The scriptures are justly styled the revealed will of God. They are addressed to all mankind and given to remain as a rule of faith and manners to the end of the world. It must, therefore, follow that whatever is necessary to be known in them is to be as easy and intelligible at one time as another and to all men alike.

Where their meaning cannot be positively determined, a new inspiration will be necessary to reduce them to certainty. And if that be wanting, everything else is but conjecture. Whoever, therefore, goes about to put a construction upon such passages in scripture and enjoins us to believe his interpretation does not demand submission to the word of God but to his own authority and imagination.

What use is there of an unintelligible proposition? Or of a revelation which wants to be revealed? Almighty God will never require of us to see in the dark till he has given us new eyes. Nor to believe any article or obey any precept till we understand him and know what he means. A rule, which is not plain, is no rule at all. Nor will he make a law binding or the transgression of it a sin till we know what it is. . . .

[God] sees our hearts, penetrates the most secret recesses of our souls, makes indulgent allowances for our weaknesses, and expects nothing from us but what he has given us the means and abilities of knowing and performing. He requires us not to make brick without straw. He judges by the intention, not the action. We cannot offend him but voluntarily, much less offer him an affront when we design respect and obedience.

The creator and preserver of mankind cannot take delight in puzzling his creatures with darkness and ambiguities, and in points too, where their souls are in danger. He is not a rigid master who would reap where he did not sow. This would be a cruel mockery, unworthy of the divine being who has brought life and immortality to light.

Nothing is plainer than the [Old Testament] law and the Gospel. Whoever says the contrary does no less than accuse the great and good God and justify wicked and willful men, whom he has left without excuse by telling them clearly what he expects from them. "What does God require of thee, O man, but to do justice, to love mercy, and to walk humbly?" said one of his prophets out of his mouth. I am very sure there is no difficulty in understanding this.

The obscure passages in scripture could not be intended for our instruction. Infinite wisdom has hid them from our eyes to be brought to light in his own time and then to answer the ends of his providence. Or perhaps to baffle our vain pride and curiosity. Who art thou, O man, who wouldst be wiser than the omniscient [and] make those things necessary, which he has not made so? [And] discover what he has thought fit to conceal and know his secrets whether he will or no? This would be to mend the scripture, to make it more useful than God has made it, to help the Holy Ghost, and to teach the Almighty how to express himself.

How absurd would it be to send cook maids and day laborers to study Aristotle and Suarez [a medieval philosopher]; to rake into the jargon of the schools; to learn all languages; examine all systems; and to discover of themselves all errors, interpolations, and mistakes. Or to do what is much more ridiculous: that is, wholly throw themselves and their salvation in most countries upon a confederacy of men who have an interest to deceive and oppress them and ever did so when they had an opportunity; who have been always at variance with one another and with themselves; and have agreed in nothing but the misleading of those who trusted them! And yet one of these must be the unhappy circumstance of the greatest part of mankind if what I have said before be not true. Which we may be sure the divine goodness cannot permit.

## *Against Creeds*

Gordon argued that Christian creeds were unnecessary. He said that if the articles in the creed were in scripture, the creed was not needed. If the articles were not in the scriptures, the creeds "depreciate and profane the divine authority" of the Holy Spirit who inspired the scriptures. Gordon further argued that the creeds were not written to edify people. Instead, they were written by intolerant, uncharitable, and wrathful clergy to increase their power and control over the laity. This excerpt comes from the *Independent Whig*, number VI, entitled, "Of Creeds and Confessions of Faith." In the 1743 edition, it is in vol. 1, pages 40-44.

I think it but justice to the goodness of God to affirm that belief or disbelief can neither be a virtue or a crime in anyone who uses the best means in his power of being informed. If a proposition be evident, we cannot avoid believing it. And where is the merit or piety of a necessary assent? If it be not evident, we cannot help rejecting it or doubting of it. And where is the crime of not performing impossibilities or not believing what does not appear to us to be true? Are men who have good eyes the more righteous for seeing? Or do they offend in seeing too well? Or do blind men sin in not distinguishing colors?

When we clearly see the connection of a proposition or know that we have God's word for it, our assent is inevitable. But if we neither comprehend it ourselves nor see God's authority for it, and yet swallow it, this is credulity and not divine faith, which can have nothing less than divine truth for its object. When we are sure that God almighty speaks to us, we readily believe him who cannot lie, nor be mistaken, nor deceive us. But when men speak, though from God himself, our belief in them is but human confidence, if we have only their own authority that they had it from God. Their being bishops, their being learned, their meeting together in synods, all this alters not the case. We can judge of their opinions no otherwise than as of the opinions of men and of their decisions but as of human decisions.

When the articles of any creed appear to be contained in scripture, whoever believes that does in consequence believe them, and then such creed is unnecessary. But when we cannot, or think we cannot, find them in scripture and yet give equal credit to them, we depreciate and profane the divine authority itself by accepting the words of man's invention as wiser and more significant than the words of God's own choosing.

We are sure that the scripture phrases were inspired by the Holy Ghost, and as sure that our own forms and injunctions are human and framed by priests. It is, therefore, strange that the former should be insufficient and unintelligible, and the latter infallible and to be embraced and obeyed on the pain of damnation. And that the priests must do what God almighty has, without success, endeavored to do.

Besides, as the imposition of human creeds is contrary to reason, so is it also to charity. They were generally made in a passion, not to edify, but to plague those for whom, or rather against whom, they were intended. They were the engines of wrath and vengeance, nor could they serve any other purpose. Those who believed them already did not want them. And those who disbelieved them were not the better for them. But this was not the worst of it. For they who did not receive them against their conscience were cursed. And they who did, deserved it. So that either the wrath of God on one hand, or the wrath and cruelty of the clergy on the other, was unavoidable. If people said they believed and did not, they mocked God and shipwrecked their souls. And if they did not believe and owned it, though they saved their souls, they provoked their reverend fathers and were destroyed....

Thus, creeds, as they were the result of revenge, pride, or avarice, were the constant preludes and introductions to ignorance, cruelty, and blood. And the wretched laity were craftily, as well as inhumanly, made the deluded and unnatural instruments of butchering one another to prove the infallibility of the faith-makers. Who, while they were wantonly shedding Christian blood and dooming to damnation those who called upon the name of the true God, had the shameless assurance to miscall themselves the ambassadors of the meek Jesus.

And indeed, what better could be expected from men so chosen, so unqualified, and so interested, as the members of these general creed-making councils for the most part were? They were chosen from several parts by a majority of votes. And they who were most aspiring, factious, or crafty carried it. They sprung from the meanest of the people. They were bred in cells [of the monks]. They popped into the world without experience or breeding. They knew little of mankind, and less of government, and had not the common qualifications of gentlemen. They were governed by passion and led by expectation. And either eager for preferment or impatient of missing it, they were the perpetual flatterers or disturbers of princes.

These were the men, this their character. When these reverend fathers were got together in a body by the order of a prince or a pope, who, having his necessities or the ends of his ambition to serve, chose proper tools for those purposes, they were directed to form such creeds and systems of faith as his present views or interests made requisite for mankind to believe.

## *Praising Reason*

Trenchard and Gordon wrote an essay together in which they described how the Christian clergy tried to stop people from using reason in religious matters. Gordon then wrote another essay in which he praised human reason calling it "a ray or impulse of the divinity," that lifted humanity "into a resemblance with God himself." Gordon argued the reason was the judge of any alleged supernatural revelation, saying that it was by reason that "we distinguish the beauty and truth of the Gospel from the imposture and absurdity of the Koran." Moreover, he said that people only left the Roman Catholic Church and embraced Protestantism because reason showed the senselessness of the Catholic doctrine of transubstantiation. Gordon argued that the only people who were against using reason in religious matters were those who wanted to keep people ignorant and slavish, such as the Muslim clergy in Turkey and the Catholic clergy in general. The first two paragraphs of this excerpt come from the *Independent Whig*, number VIII, entitled, "Of Uninterrupted Succession. Part 2." In the 1743 edition, it is in vol.1, pages 55-56. The rest of this excerpt comes from the *Independent Whig*, number XXXV, entitled, "Of Reason." In the 1743 edition, it is in vol. 2, pages 24, 26-33.

The greatest part of mankind have learned to judge of religious matters by other faculties and senses than those which God almighty has given them. The first thing they are taught is that reason may be on one side of the question and truth on the other. Which maxim being well established, there will be an end of all reasoning ever after, and there can be no longer any criterion between truth and falsehood. But those, who by education and custom, have once got possession of their superstition and fears may impose upon them what crafty and advantageous doctrines they please.

By these means, the Christian religion, most easy and intelligible in itself and adapted to the meanest capacities, is become, in most countries, a metaphysical science made up of useless subtleties and insignificant distinctions. Calculated to gratify the pride of corrupt clergymen by making them admired and reverenced by the people for their profound knowledge and deep learning. And, consequently, religion is wholly left to their care and conduct as being infinitely above poor lay apprehensions. And to this, the world is beholden for the depravation of virtue and morality and for all the domination, pomp, and riches of the popish priesthood....

Reason is the only guide given to men in the state of nature to find out the will of God and the means of self-preservation. The senses are its subordinate instruments and spies. They bring it intelligence, and it forms a judgment and takes measures, according to the discoveries which they make. It compares things one with another and chooses them, if they are good. Or neglects them, if they are indifferent. Or shuns them, if they are bad. It discovers a first cause, the maker, contriver, and preserver of all things. And, therefore, it teaches submission to his will, admiration of his wisdom and power, and thankfulness for his goodness and mercy....

Reason checks tumultuous passion, the greatest enemy to the peace of the mind and to the peace of society. Hence, it has been observed by the same moralist that all our rational pursuits are temperate pursuits and that what we pursue with reason, we never pursue with violence. Reason subdues anger and prevents cruelty. It makes a man less fierce than a lion and less ravenous than a bear. It is not human shape, but human reason that places a man above the beasts of the field and lifts him into a resemblance with God himself. Hence, it is justly styled divine *particula auræ*, a ray or impulse of the divinity. And in what sense can a man be said to be made after the image of God unless by his possessing that reason which is a divine particle of the Godhead? We resemble not our maker in person or complexion and, therefore, can only resemble him in reason and in mercy, which is the child of this divine reason.

Were we not rational creatures, we could not be religious creatures but [would be] upon a level with brutes, to whom God has made no revelation of himself because they want reason to discern it and to thank him for it. Revelation, therefore, presupposes reason and addresses itself to reason. And God himself, by persuading us as he does in his word [the Bible] by the voice of reason, appeals to our reason. We cannot glorify God but with our understandings. And we are convinced of his goodness before we adore it. To praise him, without reason, is a contradiction and an impossibility. The devotion which he requires must be free, rational, and willing, and where it is not so, it is folly or hypocrisy.

Nor is there any opposition between reason and grace, whatever some may weakly or dishonestly maintain. In truth, grace is never given but where reason was already given. And the former cannot subsist where the latter does not. We may have worldly wisdom without piety, but cannot possess piety without understanding. Nor does grace, though given in the greatest abundance, at all supply the ordinary offices of reason. We do not find that St. Luke was a better physician for having written a Gospel, or St. Paul a better sailor or better tent-maker for being an apostle. But neither could St. Luke have been an evangelist, nor St. Paul an apostle, unless God had given them reason as well as grace. Indeed, they are both the gifts of God, only the one is ordinary, and the other is extraordinary.

Reason, even without the light of revelation, teaches us to investigate nature and praise God for the wonderfulness of his works. It must judge of revelation itself, what is so, and what not; and of the words and language in which the holy oracles were at first conveyed; and of the words and language into which they were afterwards translated. Now words, many of them, being obscure or equivocal and signifying different things to different men, it is left to our reason to determine in what sense these words are to be understood. The spirit of God has invented for us no new ones or such as carry in their sound certain and determinate ideas which cannot be mistaken, but must infallibly be the same to every man.

By the light of reason, we see about us. It warns us against craft [trickery] and arms us against force. And the same reason, which commands us to believe in God implicitly and obey him passively, does also command us to trust to no man without inquiry and to submit to no man without cause. Thus, what is our duty in relation to God, would be madness in relation to one another. The good God cannot deceive us, but men have pride, folly, interest, and complexion, all conspiring to deceive themselves and others....

Pray, how do we distinguish the beauty and truth of the Gospel from the imposture and absurdity of the Koran, but by our reason? How do we detect the impudent and senseless doctrine of transubstantiation, but by our sense and reason? Why did we, or how could we, leave popery and embrace the [Protestant] Reformation, but because our own private reason told us? And scripture, of which we made ourselves the judges, told us that we left slavery, falsehood, and cruelty, for truth, freedom, and innocence? How did our Savior prove himself the Son of God but by miracles which every eye saw and every ear heard? He appealed to the sense and reason of mankind, and all were convinced that would be convinced. How do we know the scripture to be the word of God but by the deductions and information of reason? How can we prove our own church, as by law established, to be the purest and best constituted church in the world but by the testimony of impartial, disinterested reason? For it is plain, from the great number of gainsayers and Arians [Christians who deny Jesus was God], that her genuine sons have not the miraculous gift of inspiring from above all men with their own orthodox sentiments. How can we distinguish religion from enthusiasm, grace from superstition, faith from credulity, the love of the church from the love of power, and the authority of God from the impositions of men, but by reason or by the scripture interpreted by reason?

In short, all who are friends to truth are friends to reason, the discoverer and champion of truth. And none are foes to reason but those who have truth and reason for their foes. He who has dark purposes to serve must use dark means. Light would discover him, and reason expose him. He must endeavor to shut out both and make them look frightful by giving them ill names, for farther than names the vulgar inquire not.

From this cause, religion and liberty flourish where reason and knowledge are encouraged. And wherever the latter are stifled, the former are extinguished. In Turkey, printing is forbidden, inquiry is dangerous, and free-speaking is capital [crime] because they are all inconsistent with the Mahometanism [Islam] by law established. Hence, it comes to pass that the wretched Turks are all stupidly ignorant, are all slaves, all infidels. Nor have the papists much advantage to boast above the Mahometans [Muslims]. Their guides and governors lock up from them the scripture, which is the book of knowledge. They teach them that ignorance is the mother of devotion. They banish liberty. They browbeat reason. They persecute truth. In consequence of all which, the deluded votaries of the Romish Church are as ignorant as the Mahometans, as greater slaves, greater idolaters, and greater persecutors. That is, in barbarity they exceed the Turks, who in barbarity exceed most others.

Here in England, why are we free, why Protestants, but because we are guided by reason and judge for ourselves? And none amongst us complain of the liberty of the press or the growth of freethinking but those who would found a dominion upon stupidity and persecution. Vile and woeful is that cause which must be supported by ignorance and misery! And yet, there are those in Great Britain, who, though they wear a holy and venerable livery, yet have the boldness and blasphemy to christen that impious cause, the cause of God and of his church.

To conclude, scripture and reason, without which scripture can have no effect, are the only tests of every falsehood and imposture and every superstition. Suppose, for example, a reverend doctor is touched with an odd zeal for bowing to the East. He ought to convince my reason that bowing to the East is enjoined in scripture before he enjoins me to bow also. If he says that it is enjoined by the authority of the church, he then must satisfy my reason that the scripture teaches the church to teach her members to make bows. If he answers that neither does the scripture teach to bow to the East, but that the church thinks bowing decent and edifying, he must then prove, by rational evidence, that what every church thinks decent is a duty. If he replies that this is only true of the one orthodox church, then he must prove that his church is the sole orthodox church according to the rules of the Gospel.

And if the doctor cannot do this to my satisfaction, then there will be an end of his argument for his ecclesiastical bowings.

As we judge from scripture what is orthodoxy, so we must judge from reason what is scripture.

## *Against Religious Persecution*

Gordon pointed out that Jesus never used force against those who did not believe in him and neither did the apostles. They tried to convince people of the truth of Christianity either by reason or by performing miracles. Gordon asserted that Christian clergy who persecuted people "give the lie to the Lord of Life and disown him for their head." This excerpt comes from the *Independent Whig*, number XXIV, entitled, "Of Persecution." In the 1743 edition, it is in volume 1, pages 207-214.

There are but two ways of propagating religion: namely, miracles and exhortation. The one depends upon divine power and the other upon the strength of reason. Where the finger of God appears, all further testimony is needless. And where the truth is obvious to reason, miracles are needless. God never wills us to believe that which is above our reason, but he at the same time commands our faith by miracles. He does not leave necessary things doubtful, and for this reason alone it is that men are said to be left without excuse.

Every point of belief, therefore, must be supported either by reason or miracle, or else it is no point of belief at all. Both the Jewish and the Christian law were delivered and enforced with manifest signs and demonstrations of God's extraordinary presence and power. And it has been very justly boasted of the Christian religion in particular that it spread and prospered by miracles, persuasion, and clemency in opposition to violence and cruelty.

But when Christianity became tainted and defaced by priestcraft, it grew necessary to have many points believed which contradicted both revelation and common sense. Therefore, its foster fathers, who to the worship of God added the worship of themselves, had no other way to prove their system but by wrath and vengeance. Reason was against them and miracles not for them. So, their whole dominion stood upon falsehood, guarded by force. This force, when it is exercised upon a religious account, is called persecution, which is what I am now to consider and expose.

To punish men for opinions that are even plainly false and absurd is barbarous and unreasonable. We possess different minds as we do different bodies. And the same proposition carries not the same evidence to every man alike, no more than the same object appears equally clear to every eye. A choleric temper, when it is not corrected with reason and seasoned with humanity, is naturally zealous. A phlegmatic temper, on the other side, as it is naturally slow, so it is lukewarm and indifferent. Is there any merit in having a warm complexion or any sin in being dull?

But further, to punish a man for not seeing the truth or for not embracing it, is, in the first place, to make him miserable because he is already so. And in the second place, to pluck vengeance out of God's hands, to whom alone it belongs, if we will take his own word [the Bible] for it. If this severity is pretended to be for his good, I would ask: is manifest cruelty any token of kindness? Or was it ever taken for such? Does it not always increase the evil which it is employed to cure? Is destruction the means to happiness? Absurd and terrible! . . .

Our blessed Savior, who had no view but the redemption of the world, never used his omnipotence or the least force to subdue his enemies, though he knew their hearts to be malicious and implacable. He neither delivered them to death nor the devil, even for their hellish designs to kill him, much less for points of error or speculation. He reasoned with all men, but punished none. He used arguments, he worked wonders, but severities he neither practiced nor recommended. His was a different spirit. He rebukes his apostles with sharpness, when, being yet full of the spirit of this world and void of the spirit of God, they were for bringing down fire from heaven upon the heretical Samaritans. The merciful Jesus would not hurt these half-heathens, though they rejected him in person. For he "came not to destroy men's lives, but to save them." And they who take another method give the lie to the Lord of Life and disown him for their head.

His apostles, as soon as they had received the Holy Ghost, grew wiser and more merciful. They showed by miracles that they were endowed with the divine power. But they never used either to compel or to burn, though they were beset with false teachers and opposed by gainsayers. They were so far from giving ill-usage that they never returned it. The exercise of wholesome severities was no part of their doctrine. Prayers and persuasions were their only arms and such as became the Gospel of peace.

This was the mild and heavenly behavior of Christ and his apostles towards those who did not believe or believed wrong. And it was followed by all their successors who aimed at the good of souls. But those who used the sacred function as a ladder to power and gain made a new Gospel of their own decisions and forced it upon the world, partly by fighting and partly by cursing. The apostles taught Christ, and their successors taught themselves. It was not enough to believe the doctrine of Christianity, but you must believe it in words of their inventing. To dispute their decrees, though they contradicted common sense and the spirit of God, was heresy, and heresy was damnation. And when, in consequence of this, they had allotted a pious Christian to eternal flames for his infidelity in them, they dispatched him thither with all speed. Because he was to be damned in the other world, therefore he was to be hanged or burned in this. A terrible gradation of cruelty! To be cursed, burned, and damned! But it was something natural; it began from persecuting priests and ended in hell, and the devil was the last and highest executioner.

Thus, they became prelates of both worlds and proprietors of the punishments of both. Even where the civil sword was not at their command, their vengeance was as successfully, and, in my opinion, more terribly, executed without it by the temporal effect of their excommunication. For the person under it was looked upon as a demon and one in the power of the devil. And so, driven out like a wild beast from all the comforts of life and human society to perish in a desert by hunger, or the elements, or beasts of prey. And all this, perhaps, for denying a word, or a phrase, which was never known in scripture, though impudently pretended to be fetched from thence.

Such dreadful dominion had they usurped over the bodies and souls of men, and so implacably did they exercise it! And, to fill up the measure of their falsehood and cruelty, they blasphemously pretended to be serving God, when they were acting as if there were none.

Those who set up for infallibility have found a good excuse, if it were true, for the insupportable tyranny, infinite murders, and wide devastations which their religion has everywhere introduced. But those, who exact a blind obedience to decrees which they own to be human, and annex penalties to positions which we know to be false and they know to be disputable, and, in fine [in summation], act and dictate as if they were infallible without pretending to be so, are so utterly without all excuse that I know no language which affords a name proper for their behavior.

The Mahometan [Muslim] imposture was professedly to be spread by the sword. It had nothing else but that and libertinism to recommend it. But to propagate the Christian religion by terror or arms is to deny it. It owns no such spirit. It rendered itself amiable and gained ground by a principle of peace and love. These were the means instituted by Christ for the recommendation and defense of his Gospel. And they, who would choose contrary ones, charge him with folly and have ends to serve very different from his. Ambition, pride, and revenge may make good use of violence and persecution, but they are the bane of Christianity, which always sinks when persecution rises. The vilest and most profligate men are ever the greatest promoters of it, and the most virtuous are the greatest sufferers by it. Libertines stick at nothing, but they who have the fear of God cannot comply with all things.

Persecution is, therefore, the war of craft against conscience and of impiety against truth. Reason, religion, and liberty are its great foes. But ignorance, tyranny, and atheism its great seconds and support. We ought then constantly to oppose all claims of dominion in the clergy, for they naturally end in cruelty. I believe it will be hard to show that ever the priesthood, at any

## The Nature of True Christianity

In the last essay in the *Independent Whig*, Gordon and Trenchard explained their idea of the nature of true Christianity. They said that there was only one essential article of belief for a Christian—that Jesus was the Messiah. It did not matter if a person performed sacrifices, rituals, or observances or believed in Christian doctrines contained in creeds. One was a good Christian if one believed that Jesus was the Messiah and followed Jesus' teachings to love God and one's neighbor. This excerpt comes from the *Independent Whig*, number LIII, entitled, "In What Only True Religion Consists." In the 1743 edition, it is vol. 2, pages 219-223, 225-232, & 235-236.

I have undertaken in this paper to prove, what, methinks, should want no proof: namely, that the all-powerful God is not a whimsical and humorous being that governs his creatures by caprice and loads them with arbitrary and useless burdens which can serve no good purpose in nature.

The Almighty is infinitely happy in his own perfections and cannot receive pleasure from such things or actions as only the weakest men are fond of and the wisest condemn. He is not capable, like mortals, of being ruffled by accidents or surprised by disappointments. Wisdom, goodness, and felicity are essential to his being. And, consequently, he could have no view in creating mankind but their own happiness. For we can neither add to his nor take away from it.

It is absurd, therefore, to suppose that there can be any merit in bare opinions and abstruse speculations; or in the performance of indifferent and useless actions; or, indeed, that anything can be part of true religion but what has a tendency to make men virtuous and happy. The father of mercies will never perplex our minds or burden our bodies with anything that signifies nothing. . . .

It seems plain to me that there is but one article of faith in all this religion [Christianity], and that essential to the very being of it: namely that "Jesus is the Messiah." Without this preliminary acknowledgment, his mission could not have been owned nor his precepts obeyed, which are nothing else but exhortations to love and directions for social happiness and which he has enforced by annexing eternal rewards to the observance of them. Hitherto, virtue had expected its reward in this life, but our Savior gave new sanctions to it by bringing life and immortality to light.

There is no proposition in all scripture more evidently revealed or laid down in more positive and express terms than that the confession of this truth was the basis and support of Christianity, the great thing requisite to be believed. Everything else is practical duty, and belief is no farther concerned in it than as it produces practice. For before we can think ourselves obliged by a precept, we must be satisfied of its reasonableness or of the legislator's authority.

The world has been so long corrupted by superstition and deluded and abused by selfish and lying priests who taught wickedness for virtue and nonsense for philosophy, and placed devotion in foolish ceremonies and sacrifices, and in ridiculous cringes, antic vestments, and grimaces, that nothing less than a divine legislator with the power of miracles could restore men to their senses and to natural religion. The sole article, therefore, that our Savior made necessary to be believed was that he came from God and acted by the authority of God. Then, everyone would see the impossibility that he could deceive or mislead men and, consequently, would take his word for everything else in the sense which he understood it.

And this proceeding was agreeable to eternal reason: namely, to make nothing necessary in belief which was not necessary to practice. For what purpose could be served in obliging men to believe, or rather to say that they believed, mysterious and unintelligible propositions? Such articles are only the watchwords of a party [sect] and can never be the objects of real assent. For no man can be said to believe what he does not understand and has not suitable ideas of as far as his belief goes. We must understand the meaning of every term in a proposition before we can assent to it or dissent from it. For words of which we do not understand the signification are the same to us as if they had no signification at all. How much, therefore, more honest and prudent would it be to own, at first, our ignorance concerning certain abstruse speculations than to form propositions about them, pretend to define and explain them, and then confess that we do not understand our own definitions and explanations. And call out heresy and atheism, when we are desired to speak intelligibly and tell what we mean! . . .

Let us, therefore, see what are those commands in the observance of which Christianity consists. It does not consist in the observance of days, nor months, nor times, nor years . . .

It does not consist in positive institutions, in forms and ceremonies . . . It does not consist in meats nor drinks, in fish nor in flesh. . . .

It consists not in long prayers, nor in many prayers. Matthew 7.7-8: "When ye pray, use not vain repetitions, as the heathens do. For they think they shall be heard for their much speaking. Be ye not therefore like them. For the father knoweth what things ye have need of before ye ask." Indeed, it seems plain to me from this text, as well as from the reason of the thing, that prayer itself becomes chiefly a duty as it raises our minds by a contemplation of the divine wisdom, power, and goodness, to an acknowledgment of his repeated bounties to mankind. And as it disposes us to an imitation of those high perfections [of God] and to be merciful and beneficent to one another. For it is absurd to suppose that we can direct the all-wise being in the dispensations of his providence or can flatter or persuade him out of his eternal decrees. If, therefore, any texts in scripture seem to carry a contrary implication, I conceive that they ought to be understood with the same allowance as those are which speak of God's hands and feet and of his being subject to human passions. . . .

How, therefore, shall we worship him? How know his will? St. John tells us, chapter 7, verse 17: "If any man will do God's will, he will know of the doctrine, whether it be of God or not." That is as much as to say: make use of the judgment which God has given you and see whether the doctrine taught [to] you be worthy of an omnipotent author. See whether it teaches peace and love to your neighbor, compassion to all in distress, forbearance of injuries, humanity and indulgence to all who differ from you, duty to parents, submission and obedience to the laws of your country, and charitableness and benevolence to all mankind and even to the brute creation. Then, you may be sure such doctrine comes from God. But if it breathes forth revenge and implacable hatred; if it raises mobs, civil wars, and persecutions for trifling opinions; if it have for its end, ambition and worldly pride and overturns everything sacred and civil which stands in its way; if it encourages the worst men and oppresses the best; if it discourages industry and depopulates nations, then there are plain traces of Satan's or the popish priest's foot in it, and such a religion can never come from God.

When you have made this your best use of the faculties which God has given you, your endeavors will certainly be accepted by him. And you will meet all the reward which attends the judging right, since you have done all in your power to do so. For God puts upon no man the Egyptian task of making bricks without straw, nor requires anything which you cannot perform....

This comprehensive charity, this spirit of public beneficence, runs everywhere through the New Testament. Nor can I find any precept there given but what is manifestly advantageous to mankind, conducing to their present happiness, and deducible from eternal reason and the result of it. Matthew 12, verses 35-39: "A lawyer asked of our Savior, 'Which is the great commandment of the law?' And Jesus said unto him, 'Thou shalt love the lord thy God with all thy heart, and with all thy soul, and with all thy mind. This is the first and great commandment. And the second is like unto it: thou shalt love thy neighbor as thyself. Upon these two commandments hang all the law and the prophets.'"...

But the want of faith is here objected to no man. No one is rewarded or punished for believing or not believing in transubstantiation, consubstantiation, or the real presence, in predestination, or free will, or for having or not having right or wrong conceptions of the Trinity in unity, the incarnation, hypostatic union, infinite satisfaction, etc. Nor is the divine right of bishops, presbyters, and tithes once mentioned. Not a word about obedience to spiritual sovereigns and ecclesiastical princes or about our receiving the sacraments from a regular priest descended in a right line from the apostles.

Such a religion as this, which I have described, is agreeable to the divine justice which does not punish any man for speculative opinions and especially for opinions which neither do good nor hurt to anyone and for opinions which no one can help.

This is a religion every way worthy of its eternal author, and we may know by the doctrine that it comes from God. It is a religion for men of sense, for philosophers, for honest men. And comprehensible too by the meanest vulgar, without a guide. A religion of reason, free from the blind mazes and studied intricacies of popish priests and beneficial to society at first view. It despises apish gestures and external buffoonery and effectually prevents and puts an end to all inhuman fierceness and holy squabbles ever occasioned by the selfish religions of corrupt priests. It leaves not unhappy men in perpetual doubts and anxieties, nor tosses and tumbles them for relief out of one superstition into another, but esteems them all alike.

In short, this is a religion which every wise and honest man would wish to be [a] religion. A religion of charity, the religion of Jesus.

## *Against National Punishments*

The Bible said that God punished whole cities and nations, such as Sodom and Gomorrah, for their sins. (Genesis 18-19) In the eighteenth century, English Christians believed that God still punished whole countries for their sins by inflicting them with plagues, fires, and earthquakes. This belief was so widespread that when England suffered natural calamities, the government often proclaimed days of fasting, humiliation, and repentance during which people would pray to God to stop punishing their country. Gordon did not reject this idea by saying that God was too distant and inactive to ever do this. Instead, Gordon said that no one knew how God's providence worked in particular instances because wicked people often prospered while good people often suffered. Gordon thought that the only people who would ever say that a particular calamity was God punishing a person or country were people who were "fierce and uncharitable . . . ignorant and narrow-spirited bigots."

## Chapter Four

This excerpt comes from *Cato's Letters*, 4th ed., vol. 1 (London, 1737), 343-347. This is number LII, entitled, "Of Divine Judgments. The Wickedness and Absurdity of Applying Them to Men and Events."

I have in a former letter to you, not long since, shown the rashness of men in applying to one another the judgments of God. I shall in this [letter] consider that subject farther and endeavor to cure that prevailing and uncharitable spirit.

Almost all sorts of men pretend, in some instances, to be in the secrets of the Almighty, and will be finding out the unsearchable purposes of his providence. They will be prying into the hidden things of God and assigning such ends and motives for his all-wise dispensations as are only suitable to their own weakness, or prejudices, or malice. They give him the same passions that they themselves possess and then make him love and hate what and whom they themselves love and hate. They are pleased with flattery and sounds and provoked by trifles and names, and so they think is he. And as they thus sanctify all their own doings, affections, and fancies with a fiat and approbation from heaven, and belie and provoke God to make him their friend, so they take it for granted that he is an enemy to all their enemies. And that, therefore, every evil or seeming evil that befalls their enemies or those whom they dislike is a manifest judgment from God and a justification of whatever they can do against them. So, that God is often made the author of every mischief which they themselves commit. But they that feel it, think more rationally that they are animated by a contrary spirit.

God made man after his own likeness: perfect, amiable, merciful, and upright. And men are bold and foolish enough to make God after theirs. And almost everyone has his own God, one fashioned according to his own temper, imaginations, and prejudices. In this sense, they worship as many false gods as they have wrong notions of the true one. And so, in some sort polytheism does yet remain, even in the Christian world. They only agree in calling what they worship by the same name, but they conceive him in such a different manner, they differ so widely about his nature and will, and either give him such contradictory attributes, or so contradict one another in explaining these attributes, that it is plain they do not mean one and the same being. Some make God hate what he certainly loves, others make him love what he certainly hates, and all take it amiss if you think that they own and adore any God but the true God. But let them think what they will, many of them still worship the old gods of the heathens, gods that were delighted with baubles, show, and grimace, and with cruelty, revenge, and human sacrifices.

From this mistaken and impious spirit, it proceeds that when calamities and disasters befall others, especially those that differ from us, we call them "judgments" and say that the hand of God is against them. But when the same evils or worse befall ourselves, the style is changed, and then "whom God loveth he chasteneth." Or if we own them to be judgments, yet still they are judgments upon us for other people's sins.

Thus, all the misfortunes that happened to Spain for many hundred years, whether they came from the enemy or the elements, were divine judgments upon them for suffering the idolatrous Moors [Muslims from North Africa] to inhabit that good Catholic country. And, therefore, like true Catholics, they brought the greatest judgment of all upon it by destroying and banishing that numerous and industrious people. Thus, the bigoted Pagans, when Alaric, King of the Huns, sacked Rome, charged the Christians with being the cause of that and of every other calamity that befell the Empire. The Christians despised their gods, and therefore their gods, out of a particular spite to the Christians, afflicted the whole world with miseries. And so plagues, wars, hurricanes, and earthquakes, which were evils that had been in the world from the beginning of it and will be to the end, were, notwithstanding, all so many judgments occasioned by the poor Christians! Hence the beginning of penalties, severities, and persecutions against them. And thus, the Christians came in time to return the charge upon the heathens, to use the same way of reasoning, and to make the like reprisals, and with as little equity, truth, or clemency. And thus, lastly, all parties in religion have ever dealt with one another.

We are commanded "not to judge, lest we be judged," and we are told that "vengeance is the Lord's," and that judgments are in his hand. All which are to convince us that we have no certain or probable rule to apply God's judgments by and that the surest rule is the rule of charity, "which wisheth all things, hopeth all things." The good and evil that happen to man in this world are no sure marks of the approbation and displeasure of almighty God, who makes his sun to shine and his rain to fall upon the just and the unjust. Good fortune and calamities are the portion of the good and of the bad. And if there be any inequality, the wicked seem to have the advantage. The world had more people and temporal prosperity in the times of heathenism than since its abolishment. Mahometanism [Islam] possesses much more of the globe than Christianity possesses. The papists are more numerous than the Protestants are and have greater and better countries. The apostles and saints were the poorest men in the world and debauched men are often uppermost and thrive best. And as the righteous are at least as subject to distempers and affliction while they live as the wicked are, so the wicked die with as little pain and as few pangs as the righteous die.

That there is a providence and a gracious providence presiding over the world is manifest and undeniable. But how it works and from what particular motives in a thousand instances none but the author of it can tell. Though almost all pretend to tell, and are forever diving into the secret counsels of the most high, with as much temerity as ill success.

To the discredit of this practice, it is observable that none but the fierce and uncharitable, none but ignorant and narrow-spirited bigots and barbarians come into it or encourage it. Men of charitable and benevolent minds, enlarged by reason and observation, condemn it as irreligious. They know that it is often malicious and dishonest, always ridiculous and dangerous. They know the ways of God to be past finding out. They see human affairs [are] so perplexed and unaccountable. Men sometimes rising and sometimes falling, both by virtue and vice. Such vicissitudes and revolutions in the fortunes of men and of nations, often without any change in these men and nations from virtue to vice or from vice to virtue. People growing greater without becoming better and poorer without growing worse. They behold good and evil so promiscuously dispensed, sometimes thousands of men, women, and children of different spirits, merit, and morals suffering equally under the same public calamity and deriving equally the like advantages from public prosperity. They behold the adversity of some to be the visible cause of the prosperity of others, who are no better than them. And the prosperity of some the visible cause of the adversity of others, who are no worse than the former. And one and the same thing producing good and evil to those who alike deserve or do not deserve good and evil. They see so little equity or consistency in the proceedings of men. Sometimes good men exalted, without any regard had to their virtue. Sometimes wicked men cast down, without any resentment of their crimes. Sometimes good men punished for being good and wicked men raised and rewarded for being wicked. Sometimes both good and bad suffering or prospering alike. Sometimes good fortunes following the good, and ill-fortune the bad, often taking a contrary freak [course]. I say, wise and honest men, seeing all these things in this great confusion and uncertainty, find sufficient reason to be afraid of making bold with heaven and of christening by the name of its judgments any of these events and evils that afflict any part of mankind.

CHAPTER FIVE

# The Later Writings of Anthony Collins

Anthony Collins' early writings were focused on the idea that people had a right to freely express their religious beliefs. (See chapter three.) His later writings were focused on Christian prophecies and how to interpret them. He argued that the Old Testament prophecies about Jesus were not fulfilled in the literal sense but only in a figurative or allegorical sense. Many of his Christian contemporaries thought that he was a deist who was attacking Christian prophecies to destroy Christianity. Some modern scholars agree with this conclusion, while other scholars say that he was probably a sincere Christian.

## *Collins' Interpretation of Prophecy*

Collins stated that we cannot judge whether Jesus was a divine messenger from his miracles because Jesus and his apostles claimed he was the Messiah foretold by Old Testament prophecies. Therefore, his claim to be a divine messenger has to be judged on whether he actually fulfilled these Old Testament prophecies. This excerpt comes from *The Scheme of Literal Prophecy Considered . . . Religion* (London, 1726), 310-313 & 314, & *A Discourse of the Grounds and Reasons of the Christian Religion . . . Writing* (London, 1724), 6-8 & 12-13.

Had Jesus Christ come into the world as a person sent with a revelation from God of a new religion, and had he performed miracles as the credentials of his mission, he would have had a right to have been attended to and tried upon that foot. And if his doctrines and precepts had been consistent with reason, consistent with one another, and all tending to the honor of God and good of men, his miracles, with those circumstances, ought to have determined men to have believed in him. But since he claims to be the Son of God, or Messiah of the Jews foretold by the prophets, it is requisite that claim should be made out. And it is reasonable in itself, and just to him, and necessary to all those who will not take their religion upon trust, that he should be tried by examining whether this claim can be made out or no. [Bishop Thomas Sherlock says], "The argument from prophecy becomes necessary to establish the claim of the Gospel. And as truth is consistent with itself, so this claim must be true, or it destroys all others."

[Christian theologian Arthur Ashley Sykes says], "Besides, what notions of common morality must he have who pretends to come from God and declares that 'the scriptures testify of him,' if the scriptures do not testify of him? What honesty, what truth, or a sincerity must he have, who could 'begin at Moses and all the prophets and expound' unto his disciples 'in all the scriptures the things concerning himself,' if neither Moses nor the prophets ever spoke a word about him? The prophets, therefore, must be considered, and the foundation of Christianity must be laid on them, or else to avoid one difficulty, we shall be forced into such absurdities as no man can palliate [lessen], much less can extricate himself out of."

This claim must be made out to the satisfaction of the Gentile as well as the Jew. For the fundamental article of Christianity is that "Jesus is the Christ," which is to say that he is the true Messiah prophesied of in the Old Testament and promised as the Savior of the world. And, therefore, the Gentile, who would build his religion upon a proper ground and not take it upon trust, ought to try Jesus by that claim and see whether he be the person promised, that is, whether he be the Christ. [Christian Theologian] Doctor Whitby says, "Whoever came into the world, as the Messiah must come as the Messiah of the Jews because no other nation did expect or pretend to the promise of a Messiah. Moreover, whoever came as the Messiah of the Jews must at least pretend to answer the characters of their Messiah, plainly delivered by the prophets of the Jews in their authentic records, because they [the prophecies] being by the Jews received as divine oracles, they could admit no person as their promised Messiah who answered not those characters." . . .

Jesus himself . . . discoursed to all his disciples putting them in mind that before his death he told them, "That all things must be fulfilled which were written in the Law of Moses, and in the Prophets, and in the Psalms concerning him." Adding, "Thus it is written and thus it behooves Christ to suffer and to rise from the dead the third day. And that repentance and remission of sins should be preached in his name among all nations, beginning at Jerusalem."

When the people of several nations were amazed at the apostles speaking in their several tongues, and when many mocked the apostles, saying they were full of new wine, Saint Peter makes a speech in public wherein, after saying they were not drunk because it was but the third hour of the day, he endeavors to show them that this was spoken of by the prophet Joel, and he concludes with proving the resurrection of Jesus from the Psalms.

Saint Peter and Saint John tell the people assembled at the temple that "God had showed by the mouth of all his prophets that Christ should suffer and also that Jesus should come again."

Saint Peter, to justify his preaching to the Gentiles, concludes his discourse with saying, "To Jesus give all the prophets witness that through his name whosoever (that is, Jew or Gentile) believeth in him shall receive remission of sins."

Saint Paul also endeavors to prove to the Jews, in the synagogue of Antioch, that the history of Jesus was contained in the Old

Testament and that he and Barnabas were commanded in the Old Testament to preach the Gospel to the Gentiles....

In fine [summation], Saint Paul throughout his Epistles reasons in the same divine manner from the Old Testament, which, according to him, was able to make men wise unto salvation. Asserting himself and others to be ministers of the New Testament, as being ministers not of the letter but of the spirit of the Law, that is, of the Old Testament spiritually understood. And endeavoring to prove, especially in his Epistle to the Hebrews, that Christianity was contained in the Old Testament and was implied in the Jewish history and Law, both which he makes types and shadows of Christianity.

The grand and fundamental article of Christianity was that Jesus of Nazareth was the Messiah of the Jews predicted in the Old Testament. And how could that appear and be proved but from the Old Testament?...

It being evident that the claim of Jesus to the Messiahship must be made out in order to [have] a rational belief in him, the next question is: how this claim is to be made out, whether by an appeal to the Old Testament or to the mere miracles wrought by Jesus?

My resolution thereof is that the said claim ought to be made out by appealing to the books of the Old Testament, to the Law, the Prophets, and the Psalms, which books are frequently appealed to by Jesus and his apostles in this matter. For how can we know what those books say so well as from themselves?

Collins argued that the fulfillment of prophecies was a more convincing proof that someone was a divine messenger than miracles. He claimed that much "long and laborious inquiries" were necessary for someone to be convinced that a miracle had occurred centuries ago. Whereas, it was much easier to see that someone had fulfilled a prophecy. This excerpt comes from *A Discourse of the Grounds and Reasons of the Christian Religion*, 26-27, 29-33, & 37-39.

Those proofs [about the prophecies from the books of the Old Testament] have in some measure been already produced by me, and if they are valid proofs, then is Christianity strongly and invincibly established on its true foundations. It is established on its true foundations because Jesus and his apostles grounded Christianity on those proofs. And it is strongly and invincibly established on those foundations because a proof drawn from an inspired book is perfectly conclusive. And prophecies delivered in an inspired book are, when fulfilled, such as may be justly deemed sure and demonstrative proofs. And which [Saint] Peter prefers as an argument to the miraculous attestation, whereof he himself and two other apostles were witnesses [of miracles] given by God himself to the mission of Jesus Christ. His [Saint Peter's] argument seems as follows: "Laying this foundation on that prophecy [which] proceeds from the Holy Ghost, it is a stronger argument than a miracle which depends upon external evidence and testimony." . . .

Lastly, prophecies fulfilled seem the most proper of all arguments to evince the truth of a revelation which is designed to be universally promulgated to men. For a man, for example, who has the Old Testament put into his hands which contains prophecies, and the New Testament which contains their completions, and is once satisfied, as he may be with the greatest ease, that the Old Testament existed before the New, may have a complete, internal, [and] divine demonstration of the truth of Christianity without long and laborious inquiries. Whereas, arguments of another nature, such for instance as relate to the authority and genuineness of books and the persons and characters of authors and witnesses, require more application and understanding than falls to the share of the bulk of mankind. . . .

On the other side, if the proofs for Christianity from the Old Testament be not valid, if the arguments founded on those books be not conclusive and the prophecy cited from thence be not fulfilled, then has Christianity no just foundation. For the foundation on which Jesus and his apostles built it is then invalid and false. Nor can miracles said to be wrought by Jesus and his apostles in behalf of Christianity avail anything in the case. For miracles can never render a foundation valid which is in itself invalid; can never make a false inference true; can never make a prophecy fulfilled which is not fulfilled; and can never mark out a Messiah or Jesus for the Messiah, if both are not marked out in the Old Testament. Besides, miracles said to be wrought may be often justly deemed false reports when attributed to persons who claim an authority from the Old Testament, which they impertinently allege to support their pretenses. God can never be supposed often to permit miracles to be done for the confirmation of a false or pretended mission. And if at any time he does permit miracles to be wrought in confirmation of a pretended mission, we have directions from the Old Testament not to regard such miracles, but are to continue firm to the antecedent revelation confirmed by miracles and contained in the Old Testament. No new revelation, however proved by miracles, ought ever to be received unless it confirms or does not contradict the proceeding standing, true revelation. . . .

In fine, the miracles wrought by Jesus are, according to the Gospel-scheme, no absolute proofs of his being the Messiah or of the truth of Christianity. Those miracles were prophesized of in the Old Testament, like the other matters of the Gospel. And, therefore, they are no otherwise to be considered as proofs of those points than as fulfilling the sayings in the Old Testament, like other Gospel-matters and events. Or as a Boylean lecturer [George Stanhope] well expresses it, "as comprehended in and exactly consonant to the prophecies concerning the Messiah." In that sense, they are good proofs, and in that sense only. For, as I have before observed, if Jesus is not the person prophesized of as the Messiah in the Old Testament, his miracles will not prove him to be so, nor prove his divine mission. And in that sense only, Jesus himself urges his miracles to prove his being the Messiah. For when John the Baptist, who had heard in prison of the works or miracles of Christ, but yet doubted whether he was the Messiah . . . sent two of his disciples to him to know whether he was the Messiah or they were to look for another, Christ declares himself to be the Messiah by showing that the characters of the Messiah as extant in the Prophets manifestly agreed to him in these words, "Go and show John again those things which you do hear and see. The blind receive their sight, and the lame walk, the lepers are cleansed, and the deaf hear, the dead are raised up, and the poor have the Gospel preached unto them. And blessed are they who shall not be offended in me." Which characters consist of two parts, first in doing miracles, and secondly, in appearing in a low state and teaching the poor, which last was much mistaken by and gave great offense to the Jews. For as to the first, the Jews agreed to it. Neither of which would, of itself, be sufficient to prove Jesus to be the Messiah without the other. Nor both together, but as they are the characters of the Messiah in the Prophets.

Having argued that Jesus could only be seen as the Messiah if he fulfilled the Old Testament prophecies, Collins then discussed how to tell if a prophecy had been fulfilled. He argued that these prophecies were not fulfilled according to the literal sense of the prophecy, but according to a typical, allegorical, or mystical sense. This excerpt comes from *A Discourse of the Grounds and Reasons of the Christian Religion*, 39-41 & 45-48.

Of the strength or weakness of the proofs for Christianity out of the Old Testament, we seem well qualified to judge by having the Old and New Testament in our hands. The first containing the proofs of Christianity and the latter the application of those proofs. And we should seem to have nothing more to do but to compare the Old and New Testament together.

But these proofs taken out of the Old, and urged in the New Testament, being sometimes either not to be found in the Old or not urged in the New, according to the literal and obvious sense which they seem to bear in their supposed places in the Old, and, therefore, not proofs according to scholastic rules. Almost all Christian commentators on the Bible and advocates for the Christian religion, both ancient and modern, have judged them to be applied in a secondary, or typical, or mystical, or allegorical, or enigmatical sense. That is, in a sense different from the obvious and literal sense which they bear in the Old Testament.

Thus, for example, Saint Matthew, after having given an account of the conception of the Virgin Mary and of the birth of Jesus, says, "All this was done that it might be fulfilled which was spoken by the prophet, saying, 'behold a virgin shall be with child, and shall bring forth a son, and they shall call his name Immanuel.'" But the words, as they stand in Isaiah, from whom they are supposed to be taken, do, in their obvious and literal sense, relate to a young woman in the days of Ahaz, King of Judah, as will appear by considering the context. . . .

If the reader desires farther satisfaction that the literal, obvious, and primary sense of this prophecy relates to Isaiah's own son or not to Jesus, I refer him to [Christian scholars] Grotius, to Huetius, (who confirms his explication with the authority of [the Church Fathers] Eusebuis, Basil, Jerome, Cyril, Theodoret, and Procopius). . . .

Again, Saint Matthew gives us another prophecy, which he says was fulfilled. He tells us that Jesus was carried into Egypt from whence he returned after the death of Herod, "that it might be fulfilled which was spoken of the Lord by the prophet, saying 'out of Egypt have I called my son.'" Which words being word for word in Hosea, and nowhere else to be found in the Old Testament, are supposed to be taken from thence. Where, according to their obvious sense, they are no prophecy, but relate to a past action . . . [of] calling the children of Israel out of Egypt, as, I think, is denied by few. This passage, therefore, or, as it is styled, prophecy of Hosea, is said by learned men to be mystically or allegorically applied in order to render Matthew's application of it just. And they say all other methods of some learned men to solve the difficulties arising from the citation of this prophecy have proved unsuccessful.

Matthew says Jesus came and dwelt at Nazareth that it might be fulfilled which was spoken by the prophets, saying, "He shall be called a Nazarene." Which citation does not expressly occur in any place of the Old Testament, and, therefore, the Old Testament cannot be literally fulfilled therein. . . .

In fine, the prophecies cited from the Old Testament by the authors of the New do so plainly relate in their obvious and primary sense to other matters than those which they are produced to prove. [Thus] that to pretend they prove in that sense what they are produced to prove is "to give up the cause of Christianity to Jews and other enemies thereof." Who can so easily show in so many undoubted instances the Old and New Testament to have no manner of connection in that respect but to be in an irreconcilable state.

## *The Old Testament as Canon*

In the previous discussions about prophecies, Collins' views were shared by a number of his orthodox Christian contemporaries. However, he took a very unorthodox position by denying the canonical status of the New Testament. He asserted that only Jesus and his apostles had the right to declare some books scriptural. According to Collins, they declared that the Old Testament was scriptural but never said that any part of the New Testament was scriptural. Instead, the New Testament was declared to be part of scripture hundreds of years later by "weak, fallible, factious, and interested men." This excerpt comes from *A Discourse of the Grounds and Reasons of the Christian Religion*, 13-17.

Indeed, to speak properly, the Old Testament is yet the sole true canon of scripture (meaning thereby a canon established by those who had a divine authority to establish a canon, and in virtue thereof did establish a canon) as it was in the beginning of Christianity. For the books of the New Testament are all occasional books as Mr. [William] Whiston has clearly shown, and not a "digest or a system of laws for the governing church." And, I add, were not joined together in one body or collection, nor declared by any human authority to be all canonical, till the seventh century when the controversy about the last book of canonical scriptures so-called, "seems to have been brought to an end," as says the Reverend Mr. John Richardson, our most learned defender of the canon of the New Testament. They are Christian books and contain proofs of Christianity from the Old Testament; but contain Christianity itself no otherwise than as explaining, illustrating, and confirming the Christianity taught in the Old Testament. They all seem, what Grotius expressly says of the books of Luke, "piously and faithfully written, and upon subjects of great concern to salvation, and, therefore, made canonical by the church." Which was plainly an accidental event and did befall those books gradually and after long disputes about their authority and might have befallen other pious books, which, though, deemed scripture, and declared canonical by the ancients, have been since rejected as spurious and apocryphal.

It is also to be observed that our Savior, who assures us that he came to fulfill the Law and the Prophets, and not to destroy the religion of the Jews (many of whom were, long before the coming of Christ, deemed real Christians and equally to believe the Gospel or Christianity with those who were converted by the apostles), left nothing in writing to establish his new law, if it may be so-called, which was not properly a new law, but Judaism explained and set in a due light. In a word, Jews and Christians had one and the same canon of scripture. Nor would there have been any difference between them or any separation of the latter from the former with whom they continued many years in communion after the death of Jesus, if the Jews had understood the spiritual sense of their own books as declared and explained to them by the apostles, who said "none other things to any than those which the prophets and Moses did say."

In fine, Jesus and his apostles do frequently and emphatically style the books of the Old Testament the scriptures and refer men to them as their rule and canon. And Saint Paul says, "After the Christian way, which ye call heresy, so worship I the Gods of my fathers, believing all things that are written in the Law and the Prophets." But no new books are declared by them to have that character. Nor was there [as John Ernest Grabe says] "any new canon of scripture, or any collection of books of scripture made, whether of Gospels or Epistles, during the lives of the apostles." As is confessed by the knowing in antiquity and particularly by our learned Grabe and [John] Mill, who, latest of all authors, have searched, and that with great diligence, into these matters. And if Jesus and his apostles have declared no books to be canonical, I would ask, who did or could afterwards declare or make any books canonical? If it had been deemed proper and suited to the state of Christianity to have given or declared a new canon or digest of laws, it should seem most proper to have been done by Jesus or his apostles and not left to any after them to do. But especially not left to be settled long after their times by weak, fallible, factious, and interested men, who were disputing with one another about the genuineness of all books bearing the name of the apostles and contending with one another about the authority of their very different books.

## *Evil Angels*

Many Christians say that Jesus' miracles proved that he was God and that Christianity was true. A major problem for this argument was that the Bible itself stated that evil angels performed miracles. Many Christian theologians advanced arguments claiming to show how true miracles performed by God could be distinguished from those performed by evil angels. In 1726, Reverend John Green argued that there were two ways to distinguish God's miracles from the devil's miracles. The first way was that miracles performed by God were always more powerful than those done by an evil angel. Green illustrated this point by discussing the Old Testament contest between Aaron and the Egyptian magi. Green's second way was that the devil would never teach positive doctrines that have "a natural tendency to make men holy and happy." Collins responded to Green's first argument by saying that there were many times that there was no contest between miracle-workers. Collins stated that Green's second argument was inadequate because there were many doctrines in Christianity that promoted people's misery, not their happiness. Collins finished with a long quote from Thomas Morgan, another Jesus-centered deist, about why miracles alone are inadequate to show someone was a divine messenger. This excerpt comes from *A Letter to the Author of the Discourse of the Grounds and Reasons of the Christian Religion, in Answer to Mr. Green's Letters* (London, 1726), 27-35.

How then can we distinguish when God acts or does extraordinary works and when other [evil] beings do them? He [Green] says, "God can give us a certain criterion." But what is that criterion, consistently with allowing that "[evil] beings inferior to God can do miracles or extraordinary works?"

First, he [Green] says, "the works themselves furnish us with this criterion," when, in a contest between two parties doing miracles, one party "makes it appear that the power by which he has acted was superior to that of the other." Thus, he says, in the contest between Aaron and the magicians of Egypt before pharaoh and his servants, both Aaron and the magicians "changed their rods into serpents, turned the waters into blood, and brought up frogs on the land of Egypt, and so far, they were on an equal foot. But at the next meeting, such things were done by Aaron that the magicians, not being able to imitate them, it appeared that the power by which Aaron acted was superior to that of the magicians. And that such things were done by Aaron that the magicians themselves were forced to confess unto Aaron, 'This is the finger of God.'" In answer to which I say:

Firstly, that, in the example produced, there is no [general] criterion laid down by Mr. Green to judge when an extraordinary work is done by God and when not. But [Green's criterion applies] only in the case of a contest between two parties working miracles for victory. And we are left exposed to receive all the numerous attested miracles wrought among the Pagans when there were no contests. For it appears from the affair before us that the magicians not only could and did do miracles, but that they were accustomed to do them by their free and confident entering into a contest of miracles with Aaron at the command of pharaoh.

Secondly, this victory of Aaron over the magicians does no more furnish us with a criterion to judge from the works themselves that God acted by Aaron than if either Aaron or the magicians had singly, or without a contest for superiority, wrought miracles. For if beings inferior to God can do miracles, as Mr. Green supposes, how can anybody tell from the miracles themselves in a contest between two parties, one whereof continues to do miracles after the other ceases and is unable to do more, but that it is a contest between inferior beings superior to one another in power?

*Chapter Five*

Thirdly, there can be no proof that an extraordinary work is a work of God from the work itself, but a proof that no other being can do that work besides God....

Mr. Green offers you a second criterion whereby we may know when extraordinary works are the works of God. And that is contained in these words: "That extraordinary works wrought to assure us that such a doctrine is a revelation from God are to be looked on as the works of God.... when the doctrine they are wrought for the information of has a natural tendency to make men holy and happy."

To which I answer:

First, how does such criterion show any extraordinary works to be the works of God when such works may be wrought by inferior beings? Is there any contradiction in supposing that inferior beings may propose doctrines which interested men will assert to have a tendency to make men holy and happy? And by all arts and sophistry maintain and defend as the papists [Roman Catholics] do their doctrines and practices, which have the greatest tendency imaginable to make men wicked and miserable? Or even may propose doctrines, some of which, nay all, may have that real tendency?

Secondly, that if extraordinary works or miracles are then only to be looked on as the works of God "when the doctrine they are wrought for the confirmation of has a tendency to make men holy and happy," then miracles, as such, do not evince themselves to be the works of God and are no proofs of divine revelation.... For if men know that a miracle is wrought to confirm a doctrine that has a tendency to make men holy and happy, they know the doctrine has that tendency and have a demonstrative proof of the truth and divine authority of that doctrine and need no other proof. And especially not such a proof as an extraordinary work, which may be done by a [evil] being inferior to God and which has no force in itself to prove a doctrine's coming from God, but what it derives from that doctrine [which is] itself already demonstrated to be true.

Besides the rule of making miracles then a proof of a doctrine's coming from God, when the doctrines themselves have a tendency to make men holy and happy, cannot be applied in the case of Judaism and Christianity. Both which, as consisting in many respects of merely positive doctrines, some of which have objections [as these doctrines do not make people happy]. As for example, ... God's command to Abraham to sacrifice his son.... the forbidding usury [charging interest on loans], the approbation of eunuchism [castration] as the way to the kingdom of God, the discouragement of marriage and recommending the state of virginity and single life, and diverse other such matters, too long to be enumerated here.

I conclude this subject of miracles with the observations of a late, most ingenious author [Thomas Morgan]. He says, "Perhaps it may be said, that miracles are a sufficient evidence and criterion of a revelation from God—but I would feign know what miracles there are which may not be wrought by the power of some invisible evil spirits or malicious and wicked agents, at least as to appearance, and so as to impose on the spectators beyond their capacity of detecting the cheat. And which must then have, to all intents and purposes, the same effect upon them as if the miracles were true and real? If it be urged here that as God himself cannot confirm any false doctrines by miracles, so it must be inconsistent with his wisdom, truth, and goodness to suffer others to confirm any such doctrines by false and pretended miracles, and thereby impose upon mankind in a matter of such high consequence as their eternal salvation, it is easy to reply that this is arguing against fact and experience. For that a very considerable, and perhaps the far greater part of mankind, always have been and still are thus imposed on by the pretended miracles of wicked priests and the lying wonders of Satan is evident in fact. And, therefore, to maintain that this cannot be done or ought not to be suffered is not to prove the truth of doctrines by miracles, but to impeach providence and deny the perfections of God. But the truth is that the people in popish countries, or wherever miracles are in vogue, are not to blame for not detecting the cheats of juggling [deceptive] priests and designing knaves who impose on their senses. For this, perhaps, is what they cannot do. The plot may be too close and deep and the design too nice [subtle] and knavish for them. But what they are really to blame for is their receiving doctrines as true and divine upon the bare attestation of miracles as a full and sufficient proof without regard to the nature and intrinsic character of the doctrines themselves. By this means, they are often led into schemes of religion, which in their whole frame and contrivance discover the evident marks and signatures of superstition and enthusiasm or of knavery and imposture. And which, therefore, cannot be reasonably received as coming from God, even though all miracles done from the beginning of the world had been wrought to confirm them." He [Morgan] concludes with the most just remark, "that if any doctrines are received in virtue of miracles as coming from God, which doctrines are not characterized by the reason of things and the moral fitness of actions, it is plain there can be no possible guard against enthusiasm and imposture, nor any criterion, by which we may distinguish between truth and falsehood or right and wrong in matters of religion."

CHAPTER SIX

# James Pitt

Not much is known about James Pitt's early life other than that he was born around 1700 in Norfolk and worked as a schoolmaster for a while. In 1728, he was hired to write political articles supporting the positions of the British government. These articles, under the pen name of Francis Osborne, esq., appeared in the *London Journal*, England's most popular newspaper. At the same time, Pitt wrote scores of articles about his religious beliefs in the same paper using the pen names of Socrates and Publicola. All his articles were prominently featured on the front page. One scholar estimated that Pitt's articles were read or heard by a hundred thousand people, which was about one out of every fifty people in England at the time. In my book, *The Spirituality of the English and American Deists*, I show that Pitt's deist articles were even read in America, and Ben Franklin reprinted nine of them in his own newspaper. In 1731, Pitt was appointed surveyor of tobacco for London, a post that came with considerable income. In 1738, he retired from journalism and did not write anything else. He died of unknown causes in 1755.

This chapter is composed of two complete articles by Pitt. The first article was entitled "On True Religion," and it appeared in the *London Journal* on February 8, 1729. The second article was entitled "An Essay on Original Primitive Christianity," and it appeared in the *London Journal* on November 15, 1729. The first essay discusses Pitt's ideas about natural religion, while the second essay discusses Pitt's ideas about the divinely revealed religion of Christianity.

## *On True Religion*

Pitt maintained that religious leaders have always misled people into thinking that true religion involved superstitious and irrational practices and doctrines. Pitt argued that religion was reasonable and easy to understand because it was doing our duty to God and to other people. While nature and reason, in all countries and times, showed people that they should be like God and spread joy to others by being good to them, religious leaders could not get power, money, and social status by teaching this doctrine. Instead, they told people that God was "worshipped by a devout sacrifice of our own reason." Pitt countered that it was only by using their reason that people could tell whether an alleged holy book or divine messenger was really from God. Pitt also stated that any divine messenger was only restating the moral principles of natural religion.

To the people of England,
Gentlemen,

You are very sensible that most of the letters which I have sent you have been on subjects which relate to life and action and which have a manifest tendency to form your conduct and make you happy. To pursue, therefore, the same design, this shall contain thoughts upon religion, a subject in which, it is agreed, all men are infinitely concerned. About which they all anxiously inquire, and yet, which seems very wonderful, about which almost all men differ. One would think from the goodness of that being who presides over all things that religion, which is the highest duty of every man in the world, should be most plain and easy; calculated for every nation under the sun; adapted to every capacity; and suited to every circumstance and condition of life. And it must be so. For that which is justly required of all men, all men have sufficient means to discover and sufficient abilities to perform. And had not men of superior craft [religious leaders] grown wicked enough to invent damnatory systems to work up into an art and make a mystery, the highest mystery, of what is in itself the plainest thing in the world, we should not have been able to misunderstand our duty nor lose sight of that path which leads to happiness here and hereafter. But so it is, and so it has been in most ages and countries, as far as we can trace the history of them, that a few men of convenient gravity and wisdom have thoroughly deceived and absolutely governed the rest. Those who had too much sense and honesty to be so led, they knocked down. And the believing, superstitious crowd, damned if they doubted, taught not to see, dazzled by pious tricks and false miracles, and struck blind by dreams and revelations, they led where they pleased. Poor mankind! Thus deluded and thus ruined, were, by sophistry and terror, at last convinced that was damnation to use their understandings. They were harangued out of their senses and induced to believe that perfect wisdom [God] was to be pleased by the most abject folly. And perfect reason [God] to be acceptably worshipped by a devout sacrifice of our own reason, that very reason which he [God] gave us. Thus, has the Church of Rome always acted. But we shall demonstrate to you that the only way to procure the divine favor is to use your reason and that religion is the highest reason. It [religion] is answering the relation we stand in to God as our creator and governor. As our creator, we ought humbly and thankfully to acknowledge our dependence upon him for our existence and the preservation of that existence. And as our governor, we ought to obey his will. The will of God is the happiness of men. For, he being perfectly wise, good, and powerful, and having all happiness within himself, can have no selfish ends or private views. Nor could he make the world with any other design then to communicate happiness to that infinite variety of creatures which he produced, according to their several natures and capacities. The will of God then, with relation to us being the happiness of men, and religion being obedience to the will of God, it follows that doing all the good we can to men is true religion. He who promotes the happiness of men to the utmost of his power, his will is one with the will of God. He carries on the same design and, besides the pleasure inseparably annexed to good actions, is entitled to that share of happiness which God has in store for all worthy, generous, and beneficent men. This advancing the happiness of men, considered as the will of God, does, if I may be allowed the expression, consecrate our actions and make them religiously moral. For morality and religion differ only in this: that morality is acting according to the reason of things considered as such, and religion is acting according to the same reason of things considered as the will of God who made those things and from the constitution and make of which flows certain relations in life and from those relations a reason of action. This reason of action, in order to produce happiness, being everywhere the same as founded in the nature of God and the nature of men, it follows that true religion is everywhere [the] same. It is not one thing in China, another in Persia, and another in Great Britain. But one eternal, universal, unchangeable rule of life which every reasonable being has sufficient understanding to discover and sufficient abilities to comply with. For God is the father of the world, a father perfectly wise and infinitely good, and, therefore, cannot require of us anything but what he has given us powers to perform. All he commands us to do, as free intelligent agents, is to carry on his design by promoting to the utmost of our abilities the happiness of his creatures. Wherein this happiness consists, none can be ignorant. For we are all made alike and feel alike. Our natural wants are the same, and our natural enjoyments the same too. We know, by irresistible observation and experience, the difference of right and wrong, good and evil. And, in this respect, are all taught of God. Nor is there any necessity that men should come from the East, or from the West, from the North, or from the South to teach us our duty. For we know from him who instructs them, and the most barbarous nations too, the rules of justice which we ought to follow. The voice of nature, though it speaks neither Arabic, Hebrew, or Greek, yet speaks most intelligibly to every being in the universe. But this religion, so easy to be understood, will be eternally opposed by men who have an interest against it. And there is a misfortune attending it, which I am afraid will forever sink it: and that is no persons can get by it but those who practice it. This, false spiritual leaders and holy guides, in all ages and countries knew too well, and have, therefore, made it their business to hunt down reason and debase morality. The one, they call carnal, and the other, heathenish. One they represent as incapable of finding out our duty, and the other as insufficient to recommend us to the favor of heaven. But this is the greatest injustice they can do to men and the highest blasphemy against God. It is the greatest possible injury to men, who have no other power than reason to guide them in all their actions. Nor can any actions make them happy, but moral ones. By reason they must judge of all things, visible and invisible, natural and supernatural, divine and human. By this they must judge of the authority and meaning of all books, the truth of all doctrines, and the reality of all miracles. This divine principle they must never give up on any pretense whatever. For that would be putting out the light of the intellectual world. If a man should assume the high character of being sent from heaven, it is by this principle alone we can determine whether his mission be divine or not. So that the resignation or submission of our reason not only destroys natural but revealed religion too. And reflects highly upon the wisdom and goodness of the Supreme Being, who is supposed to give us reason for all the common uses of life, and [so it seems contradictory] to command us to resign and give it up in a case where we are infinitely concerned, and our eternal happiness is at stake.

Having thus laid before you, with all possible clearness, what true religion is, we have only this to add: that the religion we have been describing is the religion of nature, or the religion of reason. We have not attempted or presumed to say anything of religion supernaturally revealed, or religion by divine positive authority. Nor will it come within the design of this letter. That you must wait for till we send you our essay on true, original, primitive Christianity. For which we have the greatest reverence, and which we believe as far as a reasonable being ought to do, who never had any immediate communication with [the] deity or ever saw a miracle wrought. But as we wholly confide in the good powers of reason, we therefore, are fully assured that whatever revelation is from God, it must be a repetition and enforcement of the religion of nature or contain nothing disagreeable to it. It must oblige men, by working upon their hopes and fears, to do those things which they ought to have done by reason, without any authority at all. For nothing is more evident than this: that natural and revealed religion, both proceeding from the same all-wise, unchangeable being and designed for the government of the same creatures, must be one. God cannot be the author of contradictions, nor speak one thing by himself and another by his messengers. The voice of reason and revelation can never disagree. The very supposition of it destroys entirely the proof of any revelation at all. For how can we be sure that men speak to us from God unless we are first sure of his being and attributes and have clear ideas of his existence and character? We must, by arguments stronger than those deduced from human testimony, know what God is before we are able to distinguish his voice from that of any other being in the universe. And when we have, by reason, discovered his nature, we are to compare what we are told concerning him with what we already know of him, and so judge whether the relation be true or not. Otherwise, we believe in men, not in God. For there's a vast difference between believing what God says and what men say concerning God. The same reason which tells us God is infinitely wise and good assures us that every doctrine which is not stamped with those characters, though ushered in with all the pomp of pretended miracles and power supernatural, cannot be from him. Vain and wicked would it be in any man, under a pretense of being a messenger from heaven, to endeavor to make us believe the truth of propositions which by the evident principles of reason we know to be false. For we are more certain of the immediate perceptions of our own minds then we can be that he is a divine messenger. Besides, if we are not to stand by our reason in this case, why in any case? What is this but to introduce universal skepticism? And, for the sake of faith, to put an end to the truth of such messengership and everything else.

Thus, gentlemen, have we given you our dissertation on religion, which, if carefully attended to, will preserve you from enthusiasm on one hand and imposture on the other; will lead you into all possible happiness in this world; and prepare you for what is to come.

Yours,
Publicola

## *Essay on Original Primitive Christianity*

In the first half of this article, Pitt claimed that true Christianity was totally contained in the first sermons of Jesus and his apostles. He said that the rest of the Bible was not relevant to people's salvation as it was either "historical" (meaning historical facts) or "occasional" (meaning words or doctrines meant for a specific people on a specific occasion). Pitt also asserted that in these first sermons, Jesus' intention was only to "repeat, restore and enforce the great law of nature." In other words, Jesus was only preaching the deist message that people who loved God and were moral would go to heaven.

The second half of the article dealt with the objection that Jesus taught more than natural religion. According to the orthodox Protestant view, Jesus taught people to have faith in him. Pitt agreed that Jesus often stated that people had to have faith in him or be damned. According to Pitt, the plain meaning of Jesus' words about faith were that "he who believes not my mission cannot by divine authority be assured that God will eternally reward good men."

The happiness of the Christian world depending so much upon the right understanding and practice of Christianity, we think it our highest duty to inquire into the nature of it and lay before mankind in a short, clear, and full view the real design of Christ's coming into the world. For that in which all men are so greatly concerned ought by all men to be well understood. We shall, therefore, with no other intent than to lead the world into truth, virtue, and happiness, show them what original, primitive Christianity is. And this we shall do from the New Testament, which is allowed by all Protestants to be the sole rule of faith and practice, and from the circumstances of the world, or the state of the Jews and Pagans, when Jesus Christ came amongst them.

## Chapter Six

In reading the New Testament, we are carefully to distinguish Christ's discourses and those of his apostles to their first converts from all the other parts of that book. For in those discourses to the people, we shall find all that is necessary to be known. The rest of the Bible is either historical or occasional.

The first sermons of Christ and his apostles must contain the whole will of God in relation to the salvation of men because thousands were converted or made Christians by those sermons, which could not have been had not the sermons contained all that was necessary to make them Christians.

In these first discourses, we find nothing inculcated but the practice of moral virtue or obedience to the eternal, universal law of God written in men's hearts. Jesus Christ, who came from God, could preach no other doctrine than what was exactly agreeable to the reason of things because God, who sent him, made those things from whence that reason resulted. God is most perfect reason and goodness and cannot be supposed to have any other design in sending a messenger into the world than to induce men, by proper motives, to act agreeably to their reasonable natures and do those actions in obedience to his will and in compliance with his authority, [actions] which have a natural tendency to produce their greatest good. And which, as wise men, they ought to have done, had there been no authority in the world, nor any coercive power in the universe. Jesus Christ, therefore, the Messiah or sent of God, could come amongst us with no other intention than to repeat, restore, and enforce the great law of nature or reason of things, in conformity to which law or reason the happiness of all intelligent beings consists. This law of nature or reason is the will of God. Nor can an absolutely perfect being have any other will in relation to the several beings he has made than that they should act up to their superior distinguishing faculties and so procure the greatest possible happiness to themselves through the whole of their existence. This will of the great creator and governor of the world, Jesus Christ preached. He recommended temperance or moderation in all enjoyments: temperance, as the root of all other virtues and as the means by which we can enjoy most real, unmixed pleasure in this life. He taught the practice of justice or acknowledging in our words and actions the rights of others, by which [practice] alone, we can fully and securely enjoy our own [rights] and without which, all societies in the world must disband. He pressed upon his followers the most extensive charity and benevolence and doing all the good we can to others. And is there a pleasure upon Earth to be compared to that which arises from the sense of making other men happy? He exhorted [people] to feed the hungry; clothe the naked; relieve the oppressed; and to bear injuries, when resenting or returning of them would do more hurt than good. He taught that passive courage, or true greatness of mind, to suffer ill rather than do ill. And he pointed out the utmost pitch of the most exalted virtue when he commanded us to do good, hoping for nothing [back] again. But, as he perfectly understood human nature and knew how difficult it was to prevail on men to act abstractly from all considerations of themselves, he opened another world and promised all those who greatly suffered for virtue in this world that they should be rewarded in the next. He knew this was an encouragement for men to be resolutely good against all the charms of pleasure, profit, and honor. But then, it was to virtue only, or rather to suffering virtue, that he annexed these rewards, and to vice only that he threatened punishments. Hear this divine person, speaking of the last day or day of judgment: "Then they shall come forth. Those who have done well to everlasting life and those who have done ill to everlasting death." Happiness and misery were by him always joined to virtue and vice, not to opinions or speculations, to rites or ceremonies.

In his discourses, there are not the least traces or footsteps of any of those numberless opinions by which his pretended followers have either ignorantly or wickedly distinguished themselves. Virtue and eternal life were all he taught. In almost twenty places in the sixth [chapter] of Saint John's Gospel, he says, for an encouragement to his virtuous disciple, "I will raise him up at the last day." Jesus and the resurrection were what Saint Paul preached at Athens. Jesus, the great teacher and example of virtue and the resurrection to reward those who steadily adhere to the practice of it through the whole course of their lives. St Peter's sermons were repentance and a good life. And the last words Christ said to his apostles before he left the world were: "Go, in my name and preach repentance and remission of sins." By repentance, in the Bible is always meant a change of life and manners: leaving off vice and constantly practicing virtue. The consequence of which will, by the favor of God, be eternal life. This is the substance and design of the whole Gospel. Nor is there the least stress laid upon anything else but obedience to the moral law or acting up to the reason of our minds. He is the author of eternal salvation to all those who obey him. Again, if our hearts or the reason of our minds condemn us, God will condemn us also. But, if our hearts condemn us not, then have we confidence towards God. So that true Christianity is following the great law of reason or acting always according to our opinion and judgment of things—after we have taken due pains to inform ourselves. This law of reason Jesus Christ came to rescue out of the hands of the Jewish and Pagan priests, who had introduced universal corruption, overwhelmed the world with their several superstitions, and made void the commandments of God by their traditions. He preached deity and virtue, against the priests of those times who, in their turns, cried out against him: "The Temple of the Lord, and sacrifices." But he went on with his glorious design of making men good and happy by preaching one God, the father of the world, and assuring us that we should find our happiness in obedience to his laws. This doctrine did Jesus preach and nothing else.

We are very sensible there will be one objection made to this discourse. It is this: did Christ preach only belief in one God and the practice of virtue? Was he only the great restorer of natural religion? Did he not preach faith also and show the necessity of it in order to [attain] salvation? Did he not say: "Unless you believe that I am he, you shall die in your sins?" Is it not said: "Without faith it is impossible to please God?" And, "He that believeth not, shall be damned." With a great variety of texts to the same purpose? In short, does not the whole Bible speak of faith as absolutely necessary to salvation? How is it then, that Christ preached only deity and virtue?

We desire that the answer we make to this objection may be carefully attended to, and then it will plainly appear to be of no force against what we have advanced, but to coincide and strike in fully with it. Attend then, for the right understanding of Christianity depends very much upon the true meaning of the word "faith." We freely acknowledge that faith is everywhere in the New Testament recommended as necessary to salvation. But then, it is faith of a moral nature; not a set of speculative opinions; not faith absolutely considered in itself, but faith as it relates to virtue. In a word, the faith of which such high things are spoken in the Bible is a belief, a firm unshaken belief, of the providence of God. A full and strong persuasion that God will, in this world or the next, make it the interest of every man to be thoroughly virtuous. It is a belief that the wise and good governor of the world has so ordered all things that justice shall be done to every being in the universe and that good men shall be finally happy. This is the only soul-animating faith. This is the faith which cherishes and keeps virtue warm. This is the faith which enabled the ancient worthies, mentioned by the author to the Hebrews [St. Paul], "To subdue kingdoms, work righteousness, obtain promises, stop the mouths of lions, quench the violence of fire, and endure tortures without accepting deliverance." And not unintelligible dry speculations about the essence of God or the nature of Jesus Christ. It was this belief that there was an external and exceeding weight of glory kept in store for good men, that they should have a kingdom which could not be moved, [and] a city which has foundations whose builder and maker is God, that made those brave men of old triumph over the united malice of Earth and hell, and not systems of mysterious words. No [Church] Councils had then met, nor were the [Church] Fathers born. And if the one had never met, nor the other ever been born, would any man be so profane as to affirm that our Christian faith had been less perfect? Or say of the [Church] Councils and [Church] Fathers, what Cardinal Pallavicini once said of Aristotle: "that had it not been for him we had lost several of the articles of our faith." No. Abhor this doctrine and the propagators of it. Believe not in men, but in God alone. This faith in God reason commands, and this is all which Christianity obliges you to. For when Christ says, "To believe in God, believe also in me," and, "Unless you believe that I am he, you shall die in your sins," and, "He who believes not shall be damned," the plain meaning is: he who believes not my mission cannot by divine authority be assured that God will eternally reward good men. So that if he fails in the practice of virtue, through the want of this strong and powerful motive, he will consequently lose that happiness which God promised by me to virtuous men only. This faith in Jesus Christ, as the Messiah, or sent of God, is a supernatural means of believing in God, or acknowledging the truth of this practical proposition: that God will finally make good men happy. And that this is so, appears from the nature of his mission and the constant tenor of his doctrine. He was sent of God to command men to do those things by divine authority, which, had they been wise, they would have done before by mere reason. He came to enforce the great law of nature by the doctrine of immortality. And assuring men that the wise and good governor of the world will so justly dispose all things that every man shall find his happiness in acting up to the laws of reason. But this authority of God must be submitted to and his mission acknowledged. Otherwise, this premise of happiness in another world would have no force. They could not obey the moral law by looking to this recompense of reward set before them without acknowledging this divine authority. Nor could they acknowledge this divine authority without acknowledging his mission. Consequently, belief in him as the Messiah was absolutely necessary to believe in God as the great rewarder in another world of those who followed the laws of reason in this.

Thus, we have laid before you what appears to be true, original, primitive Christianity, and endeavored to restore what has been, by the wickedness of the Church of Rome, so many hundreds of years lost. All wise and good men long for that blessed time when Christianity shall be thus taught. This would be the shortest way of converting deists and infidels. This would be the happy means of uniting all the different sects of Christians. This would put an everlasting end to that fierce and bloody contention about opinions, which has made more dreadful havoc in the world than all our natural evils put together. And this would introduce the peace among men, which Jesus Christ meant, when he said,

"Peace I leave with you, my peace I give unto you." That is peace arising from the consciousness of our integrity and standing well in the favor of God and all good men.
    Socrates

CHAPTER SEVEN

# The Later Writings of Matthew Tindal

The first chapter discussed how Matthew Tindal was a fellow of Oxford University and a lawyer. In the late 1600s and early 1700s, he wrote books and pamphlets criticizing his contemporaries' view of Christianity. In 1730, he published his magnum opus, *Christianity as Old as Creation*. In this book, he focused more on presenting his ideas about natural religion and its relationship to Christianity. This book was very influential, and it is often called "the deists' Bible."

All these excerpts come from *Christianity as Old as Creation*, vol. 1 (London, 1730). This book is presented as a dialogue. In the original version, Tindal designated the person representing the orthodox Christian view as "B" and the person representing his own views as "A." To make it easier to follow the argument, I changed the "B" to "CHRISTIAN" and the "A" to "TINDAL."

## *Christianity as Old as Creation*

In this first excerpt, Tindal described natural religion, which was also known as the "law of nature." In the early modern period, it was thought that natural religion was known by people's natural human faculties and did not require the supernatural light of a divine revelation. For this reason, natural religion was called the "light of nature." Part of natural religion was the moral rules or moral laws that all religions have in common. Tindal said that any alleged divine revelation must be judged by the moral principles of natural religion. This alleged revelation is only a divine revelation if it agreed exactly with the teachings of natural religion. This excerpt comes from pages 11-21, 60-61, & 67.

TINDAL: There has, no doubt, been a great number of traditional religions succeeding one another. And as far as we know, there is no traditional religion which, except in name, has continued the same for any long time. And though there are a great number of [Christian] sects who go under the same common denomination, yet they are almost as much divided among themselves as if they owned different religions and, accordingly, charge one another with erring fundamentally. Yet all these [different religions] agree in acknowledging a "law of nature," and [agree] that they are indispensably obliged to obey its dictates. So that this "light of nature," like that of the sun, is universal. And would, did not men shut the eyes of their understanding or suffer others to blind them, soon disperse all these mists and fogs which arise from false traditions or false interpretations of the true tradition.

CHRISTIAN: That we may the better know whether the "law" or "religion of nature" is universal, and the Gospel a republication of it and not a new religion, I desire you will give a definition of the "religion of nature."

TINDAL: By "natural religion," I understand the belief of the existence of a God, and the sense and practice of those duties which result from the knowledge we, by our reason, have of him and his perfections, and of ourselves and our own imperfections, and of the relation we stand in to him and to our fellow creatures.

So that the "religion of nature" takes in everything that is founded on the reason and nature of things. . . .

I suppose you will allow that it is evident by the "light of nature" that there is a God. Or in other words, a being absolutely perfect and infinitely happy in himself, who is the source of all other beings, and that what perfections soever the creatures have, they are wholly derived from him.

CHRISTIAN: This, no doubt, has been demonstrated over and over. And I must own that I can't be more certain of my own existence than of the existence of such a being.

TINDAL: Since, then, it is demonstrable there is such a being, it is equally demonstrable that the creatures can neither add to or take from the happiness of that being. And that he could have no motive in framing his creatures or in giving laws . . . but their own good.

To imagine he created them at first for his own sake and has since required things of them for that reason is to suppose he was not perfectly happy in himself before the creation. And that the creatures, by either observing or not observing the rules prescribed them, could add to or take from his happiness.

If, then, a being infinitely happy in himself could not command his creatures anything for his own good; nor an all-wise being [command] things to no end or purpose; nor an all-good being [command] anything but for their good, it unavoidably follows nothing can be a part of the divine law but what tends to promote the common interest and mutual happiness of his rational creatures. And everything that does so must be a part of it.

As God can require nothing of us but what makes for our happiness, so he, who can't envy us any happiness our nature is capable of, can forbid us those things only which tend to our hurt. And this we are as certain of as that there is a God infinitely happy in himself, infinitely good, and wise. And as God can design nothing by his laws but our good, so by being infinitely powerful, he can bring everything to pass which he designs for that end. . . .

In short, considering the variety of circumstances men are under, and these continually changing, as well as being for the most part unforeseen, it is impossible to have rules laid down by any "external" revelation for every particular case. And, therefore, there must be some standing rule, discoverable by the "light of nature," to direct us in all such cases.... Or, in other words, we can't but know if we in the least consider, that whatever circumstances men are placed in by the universal cause of all things, that it is his eternal and immutable will by his placing them in these circumstances that they act as these require. It is absurd to imagine that we are obliged to act thus in some cases, and not in others, when the reason for acting thus in all is the same. This consideration alone will direct a man how to act in all conditions of life, whether "father, son, husband, servant, subject, master, king, etc." Thus, we see how the reason of things, or the relation they have to each other, teaches us our duty in all cases whatever. And, I may add, that the better to cause men to observe those rules which make for their mutual benefit, infinite goodness has sown in their hearts seeds of pity, humanity, and tenderness which, without much difficulty, cannot be eradicated. But nothing operates more strongly than that desire men have of being in esteem, credit, and reputation with their fellow creatures. [This is] not to be obtained without acting on the principles of natural justice, equity, benevolence, etc.

In a word, as a most beneficent disposition in the Supreme Being is the source of all his actions in relation to his creatures, so he has implanted in man, whom he has made after his own image, a love for his species, the gratifying of which in doing acts of benevolence, compassion, and good will, produces a pleasure that never satiates. As on the contrary, actions of ill nature, envy, malice, etc. never fail to produce shame, confusion, and everlasting self-reproach.

And now let anyone say, how is it possible God could more fully make known his will to all intelligent creatures than by making everything within and without them a declaration of it, and an argument for observing it.

Having thus discovered our duty, we may be sure it will always be the same. Since inconstancy, as it argues a defect either of wisdom or power, can't belong to a being infinitely wise and powerful. What unerring wisdom has once instituted can have no defects, and as God is entirely free from all partiality, his laws must alike extend to all times and places.

From these premises, I think, we may boldly draw this conclusion: that if religion consists in the practice of those duties that result from the relation we stand in to God and man, our religion must always be the same. If God is unchangeable, our duty to him must be so too. If human nature continues the same, and men at all times stand in the same relation to one another, the duties which result from those relations must always be the same. And, consequently, our duty to God and man must, from the beginning of the world to the end, always be the same, always alike plain and perspicuous, and can neither be changed in whole or in part. Which demonstrates that no person, if he comes from God, can teach us any other religion or give us any precepts, but what are founded on those relations. "Heaven and earth shall sooner pass away, that one tittle of this eternal law shall either be abrogated or altered."

To sum up all in a few words, as nature teaches men to unite for their mutual defense, and government was instituted solely for this end, so to make this more effectual, religion, which reaches the thoughts, was wholly ordained. It being impossible for God, in governing the world, to propose to himself any other end than the good of the governed, and, consequently, whoever acts what is best for himself, both in a public and private capacity, does all that either God or man can require. Thus, from the consideration of our own imperfections, which we continually feel, and the perfections of our creator, which we constantly view in all his works, we may arrive to the knowledge of our duty, both to our creator and fellow creatures. Hence, I think we may define true religion to consist in a constant disposition of mind to do all the good we can and thereby render ourselves acceptable to God in answering the end of his creation. . . .

I desire no more than to be allowed that there's a religion of nature and reason written in the hearts of every one of us from the first creation by which all mankind must judge of the truth of any instituted [revealed] religion whatever. And if it varies from the religion of nature and reason in any one particular, nay, in the minutest circumstance, that alone is an argument which makes all things else that can be said for its support totally ineffectual. If so, must not natural religion and external revelation, like two tallies, exactly answer one another, without any other difference between them but as to the manner of their being delivered? And how can it be otherwise? Can laws be imperfect where a legislator is absolutely perfect? Can time discover anything to him which he did not foresee from eternity? And as his wisdom is always the same, so is his goodness, and, consequently, from the consideration of both these [points] his laws must always be the same. Is it not from the infinite wisdom and goodness of God that you suppose the Gospel a most perfect law, incapable of being repealed, or altered, or of having additions? And must not you own the law of nature as perfect a law, except you will say that God did not arrive to the perfection of wisdom and goodness till about seventeen hundred years since [the creation of the world]. . . .

The reason why the law of nature is immutable is because it is founded on the unalterable reason of things. But if God is an arbitrary being and can command things merely from will and pleasure, some things today and others tomorrow, there is nothing either in the nature of God or in the things themselves, to hinder him from perpetually changing his mind. If he once commanded things without reason, there can be no reason why he may not endlessly change such commands. . . .

Whereas, if we allow the light of nature sufficient to enable us to judge rightly in these matters, and consequently to distinguish truth from falsehood, we must own, since there can be no disagreement in truth, that there's an exact conformity between internal and external revelation, with no other difference but as to the manner of their being revealed. Or, in other words, that the Gospel, since it is impossible for men at the same time to be under different obligations, can't command those things which the law of nature forbids, or forbid what that [law of nature] commands. Nor can anything be a part of religion by one law, which by the other is superstition. Nor can external revelation make that the will of God which the light of nature continually represents as unworthy of having God for its author.

After describing natural religion, Tindal described the relationship of Christianity to natural religion. He thought that true Christianity was nothing more than a restatement of the principles of natural religion. This excerpt comes from pages 3-9.

CHRISTIAN: Surely, sir, this must be extremely heterodox. Can you believe that natural and revealed religion differ in nothing, but the manner of their being conveyed to us?

TINDAL: As heterodox as I may seem at present, I doubt not. But by asking you a few questions [I am able] to let you see I advance nothing in either of these points without reason. And to [do] it, I desire to be informed, whether God has not, from the beginning, given mankind some rule or law for their conduct? And whether the observing that did not make them acceptable to him?

CHRISTIAN: There can be no doubt, but the observing such a law must have answered the end for which it was given and made men acceptable to God.

TINDAL: What more can any external revelation do than render men acceptable to God? Again, if God, then, from the beginning gave men a religion, I ask, was that religion imperfect or perfect?

CHRISTIAN: Most perfect, without doubt. Since no religion can come from a being of infinite wisdom and perfection but what is absolutely perfect.

TINDAL: Can, therefore, a religion absolutely perfect admit of any alteration or be capable of addition or diminution and not be as immutable as the author of it? Can revelation, I say, add anything to a religion thus absolutely perfect, universal, and immutable? Besides, if God has given mankind a law, he must have given them likewise sufficient means of knowing it. He would, otherwise, have defeated his own intent in giving it. Since a law, as far as it is unintelligible, ceases to be a law. Shall we say that God, who did the forming [of] human understanding, as well as his own laws, did not know how to adjust the one to the other?

If God, at all times, was "willing all men should come to the knowledge of his truth," could not his infinite wisdom and power, at all times, find sufficient means for making mankind capable of knowing what his infinite goodness designed they should know?

CHRISTIAN: I grant you that God was always willing that all men should come to the knowledge of true religion. And we say that the Christian religion, being the only true and absolutely perfect religion, was what God from the beginning designed for all mankind.

TINDAL: If so, it follows that the Christian religion has existed from the beginning and that God, both then and ever since, has continued to give all mankind sufficient means to know it. And that it is their duty to know, believe, profess, and practice it. So that Christianity, though the name is of a later date, must be as old and as extensive as human nature, and as the "law of our creation," must have been then implanted in us by God himself.

CHRISTIAN: It would be too presuming in us poor mortals to pretend to account for the methods providence takes in relation to the discovery of its will, and, therefore, a person of less moderation might condemn your questions as captious [making petty objections], presumptuous, and founded in heterodoxy.

TINDAL: If God never intended mankind should at any time be without religion, or have false religion, and there be but one true religion which all have been ever bound to believe and profess, I can't see any heterodoxy in affirming that the means to affect this end of infinite wisdom must be as universal and extensive as the end itself. Or that all men, at all times, must have had sufficient means to discover whatever God designed they should know and practice. I do not mean by this that all should have equal knowledge, but that all should have what is sufficient for the circumstances they are in.

CHRISTIAN: Since you have asked me questions, let me, in my turn, demand of you, what are your sentiments in this matter? Particularly, what are those means which you suppose

God has, at all times, given the whole race of mankind to enable them to discover what he wills them to know, believe, profess, and practice?

TINDAL: I asked you those few questions at present, not to determine the point, but only to let you see you had no reason to be surprised at my saying, "natural and revealed religion only differ as to the manner of their being communicated." I shall now readily answer your questions. And, as I think it my duty never to disown my religious sentiments, so I freely declare that the use of those faculties by which men are distinguished from brutes is the only means they have to discern whether there is a God, and whether he concerns himself with human affairs, or has given them any laws, and what those laws are? And as men have no other faculties to judge with, so their using these after the best manner they can must answer the end for which God gave them and justify their conduct. For if God will judge mankind as they are accountable, that is, as they are rational, the judgment must hold an exact proportion to the use they make of their reason. And it would be in vain to use it, if the due use of it would not justify them before God. And men would be in a miserable condition, indeed, if whether they used it or not, they should be alike criminal. And if God designed all mankind should at all times know what he wills them to know, believe, profess, and practice, and has given them no other means for this but the use of reason, reason, human reason, must then be that means. For as God has made us rational creatures, and reason tells us that it is his will that we act up to the dignity of our natures, so it is reason [which] must tell when we do so. What God requires us to know, believe, profess, and practice, must be in itself a reasonable service. But whether what is offered to us as such be really so, it is reason alone that must judge. As the eye is the sole judge of what is visible, the ear of what is audible, so reason of what is reasonable. If, then, reason was given men to bring them to the knowledge of God's will, that must be sufficient to produce its intended effect, and can never bring men to take that for his will which he designed, they, by using their reason, should avoid as contrary to it. . . .

CHRISTIAN: If God was always willing that "all men should come to the knowledge of his truth," and there never was a time when God intended men should have no religion, or such an imperfect religion which could not answer the end of its being instituted by an infinitely wise legislator, this seems to my bewildered reason to imply that there was from the beginning but one true religion which all men might know was their duty to embrace. And if this is true, I can't well conceive how this character can consist with Christianity without allowing it, at the same time, to be "as old as the creation." And yet, notwithstanding all these seeming difficulties, I am confident the Christian religion is the only true religion. But since these difficulties are of your raising, I may, in justice, expect that you should solve them.

TINDAL: This, I must own, is a difficult point. However, I shall tell you my sentiments, which, I, far from being a "dogmatizer," am ready to give up if you can frame any other hypothesis not liable to the same objections or others equally strong. Though, I may venture to say that I take mine to be the only one which can give any tolerable satisfaction to your present doubts. And, therefore, I shall attempt to show you that men, if they sincerely endeavor to discover the will of God, will perceive that there is a "law of nature " or "reason," which is so called as a law which is common or natural to all rational creatures. And that this law, like its author, is absolutely perfect, eternal, and unchangeable. And that the design of the Gospel was not to add to or take from this law, but to free men from that load of superstition which had been mixed with it, so that true Christianity is not a religion of yesterday, but what God at the beginning dictated and still continues to dictate to Christians as well as others. If I am so happy to succeed in this attempt, I hope not only to fully satisfy your doubts, but greatly to advance the honor of external revelation by showing the perfect agreement between that and internal revelation. And by so doing, destroy one of the most successful attempts that has been made on religion by setting the laws of God at variance.

But first, I must premise, that in supposing an external revelation, I take it for granted that there's sufficient evidence of a person being sent from God to publish it. Nay, I further own that this divine person, by living up to what he taught, has set us a noble example. And that as he was highly exalted for so doing, so, we, if we use our best endeavors, may expect a suitable reward. This, and everything of the same nature, I freely own, which is not inconsistent with the law of God being the same, whether internally or externally revealed.

Tindal reviewed the recent Christian scholarship about the biblical manuscripts. This scholarship showed that there were thousands of manuscripts that often disagreed with each other. Furthermore, some of these disagreements concerned very important Christian doctrines. In the following excerpt, Tindal first quoted one of these Christian biblical scholars who summarized this scholarship. Tindal then drew the conclusion that people could not just accept everything in the Bible as an accurate record of God's activities in the world. Instead, people should only accept those parts of the Bible that showed God as acting in a totally good and fair way because natural religion showed that God was always perfectly good and fair to everyone. This excerpt comes from pages 329-330 & 327-328.

TINDAL: We, certainly, ought to adhere strictly to the light of nature if, as a learned and reverend critic [Stephen Nye] observes: "It must be allowed by the judicious and impartial that many corruptions are found in our present copies of the holy Bible. And that we have not now this blessed book in that perfection and integrity that it was first written. It is altered in many places and in some [places] of the greatest moment. I could prove, I think, by undeniable and unavoidable instances what Mr. Gregory of Oxford says in his preface to some critical notes on the scripture that he published. There is no author whatsoever, says this learned critic, that has suffered so much by the hand of time as the Bible has." If this, I say, must be allowed, ought we not in order to prevent all mistakes, in the first place to get clear ideas of the moral character of the divine being. And when by reasons much stronger than any drawn from human tradition, we have discovered this character, ought we not to compare what we are told of him [in scripture] by what we already know of him, and so judge of what men teach us concerning God by what God himself teaches us? For "we are all taught of him," and then we shall be as certain as there is a God perfectly wise and infinitely good that no doctrines can come from him that have not these characters stamped on them. Thus, were there more false readings crept into the scripture than these divines suppose, yet we might still know our duty and be certain that by doing our best to promote our mutual happiness, we answer the end of our creation. And that if we deviate from this rule for the sake of what depends on human tradition, we quit certainty for that which is not pretended to amount to more than probability....

For my part, I think that... the best way not to be mistaken is to admit all for divine scripture that tends to the honor of God and the good of man and nothing which does not. This clue, I think, will extricate the learned as well as unlearned out of many otherwise insuperable difficulties and make the laws of God, which way soever revealed, entirely to agree. And destroy that absurd notion of God's acting arbitrarily and commanding for commanding's sake. And does not St. Paul suppose no scripture to be divinely inspired but "what is profitable for doctrine, for reproof, for correction, for instruction in righteousness?" And if this be the test, ought we to admit anything to be written by inspiration, though it occurs ever so often in scripture, till we are certain it will bear this test? And, indeed, was it otherwise, we should be in a sad condition, since there's scarce any opinion, though ever so absurd or ridiculous, but has its vouchers who quote texts on texts for its support. Good lord! What a load have the different parties sects laid on it [scripture] by their not observing this rule?

But could we suppose any difference between natural and traditional religion to prefer the latter would be acting irrationally.

Orthodox Christians maintain that God made humanity perfect, but because of Adam and Eve's sin, humanity was afflicted with original sin. Original sin caused such a deep corruption of people's nature and reason that people were not able to know their duties to God and thus know how to get to heaven. It was not until Jesus' time that people knew how to get to heaven. Many orthodox Christians also asserted that people who were not Christians were doomed to hell. Tindal thought this was very unfair to people who lived before Jesus' time or who had never heard about Jesus. Tindal asserted that this portrayed God as less than perfectly good and fair and so could not be true. Instead, according to Tindal, God gave everyone an equal chance to get into heaven. This excerpt comes from pages 399 & 409-410.

TINDAL: But could we suppose a God of infinite perfection might ordain an imperfect or insufficient rule for the actions of his creatures? Or, which comes to the same [thing], afford them no other light for the discovery of it but what had such undeniable defects as made them incapable of knowing their duty? Nor was sufficient to hinder them from falling into and continuing from age to age in a deplorable state of corruption? I would ask whether God did this knowingly, or ignorantly not foreseeing the consequences? To suppose the first is to make God act out of spite and hatred to his creatures in bringing them into being and making that being a curse to them. Or, if the last, why were not these defects supplied as soon as discovered? Or were they not discovered by infinite wisdom till these latter times? And then revealed only to a small number, though all mankind had equal need of them? And then, too, so imperfectly [revealed by Jesus] that men have ever since been in continual quarrels about the meaning of most of those things which are supposed to have been added to supply the defects of the law of nature....

Can God, who equally beholds all the dwellers on Earth free from partiality and prejudice, make some people his favorites without any consideration of their merit and merely because they believe certain opinions taught in that country where they happen to be born? While others, far the greater number, shall, from age to age, want this favor not upon the account of their demerits but because [they were] destined to live in places where God, who always acts from motives of infinite wisdom and goodness, thought it best to conceal from them all such opinions. What can more represent God as an arbitrary and partial being then, thus, to suppose that he vouchsafes not to afford the greatest part of mankind the happiness of which himself had made them capable?

Must not everyone perceive that this narrow notion is inconsistent with the character of a being of unlimited benevolence? Is not infinite goodness always the same? How, then, can it in these last days make such inequality among men? Is not this supposing inconsistency in the divine conduct? Is not this notion repugnant to the natural idea we have of the divine goodness? As likewise [repugnant] to those express texts of scripture which declare "God is no respecter of persons," and that "Everyone, of what nation so ever, shall be rewarded according to his works?" and that "Men are accepted according to what they have, and not according to what they have not?"

If God, as the Doctor [Samuel Clarke] contends, will judge men as they are accountable, that is, as they are rational, must not the judgment of the most righteous judge [God] hold an exact proportion to the use they have made of their reason? And if men's state in this life be a state of probation and for that cause they are made moral agents capable of knowing good from evil, and consequently, of doing everything that's fit to be done, must they not be dealt with hereafter according to the use they have made of their moral agency?

How can men be sure, if God acts thus partially, that this partiality may not even now be in favor of other countries than those they live in, and of other notions which, not flowing from the nature and reason of things, we may be wholly unacquainted with? If men may lose any part of God's favor for impossibilities or not observing such rules as he never gave them, where shall we stop? Could I think God so partial and prejudiced as most [Christian] sects, for their own sakes, represent him, how could I admire, love, and adore him, as I ought? Nay, how can any who have such unworthy notions of God be certain God's prejudice and partiality will be in their favor? If you admit any one imperfection in God, how can you be sure of his veracity, immutability, or any other perfection whatever?

Tindal believed that people who thought that their supernaturally revealed religion was the only one true religion became intolerant. He also thought this idea led people to try to force others to believe in their religion. This excerpt comes from pages 412-413.

TINDAL: The contrary [to the idea that all good and moral people go to heaven] is a notion which lays a foundation for everlasting persecution: for if men flatter themselves that they, upon the account of their particular systems, are the favorites of heaven, and that others shall want, even to eternity, many degrees of their happiness, will not that oblige them, as they love their children, families, friends, neighbors, and relations, to use any means [and] come into any persecuting measures to prevent such opinions from spreading as they imagine would deprive them of that degree of happiness which otherwise they might ever enjoy? And is it not chiefly owing to this absurdity that even the most moderate of the different sects are far from treating one another with that benevolence which the common ties of humanity require.

Did men believe that all who were equally sincere were equally acceptable to God, there could be no pretense for the least partiality much less for persecution, either positive or negative. Nor could any man love another the less for the widest difference in opinions. And, then, of course, men's indignation would be wholly bent against immorality, discoverable by the light of nature, which, now, alas! is but too often protected by zeal for mere speculations.

This principle, and this alone, would cause universal love and benevolence among the whole race of mankind. And did it prevail, must soon produce a new and glorious face of things or, in the scripture phrase, "a new heaven, and a new Earth." And would free men from that miserable perplexity in which the fear of mistaking in speculative matters involves them.

The last excerpt from Tindal shows how he was ecstatic and transported with joy when he thought about how wonderfully God cared for humanity. Tindal also asserted that if people lived a pure and righteous life, they could "live the life of God" and could "be made partakers of the 'divine nature, be born of God, and be perfect as our heavenly father is perfect.'" This excerpt comes from pages 15 & 23-25.

TINDAL: From the consideration of these perfections [of God], we cannot but have the highest veneration, nay, the greatest adoration and love for this Supreme Being. Who, that we may not fail to be as happy as possible for such creatures to be, has made our acting for our present to be the only means of obtaining our future happiness and that we can't sin against him, but by acting against our reasonable natures. These reflections, which occur to everyone who in the least considers, must give us a wonderful and surprising sense of the divine goodness, fill us with adoration, transport, and ecstasy (of which we daily see among contemplative persons [some] remarkable instances) and not only force us to express a never-failing gratitude in raptures of the highest praise and thanksgiving, but make us strive to imitate him in our extensive love to our fellow-creatures. And, thus, copying after the divine original and taking God himself for our precedent, must make us like unto him, who is all perfection and all happiness and who must have an inexhaustible love for all who thus endeavor to imitate him. . . .

If the perfection, and consequently the happiness of God, consists in the purity and rectitude of his nature, we, as far as we can arrive to a like purity and rectitude, must be so far necessarily happy. Since by living according to the rules of right reason, we more and more implant in us the moral perfections of God from which his happiness is inseparable. We then, if I may so say, "live the life of God." That is, we, in our place and station, live after the same manner and by the same rules as he does in his, and we do what God himself would do was he in our place. And there would be no other difference between his life and ours, but what arises from our different states and relations. Since the same rules would determine our wills as determine his will. And by our repeated acts of virtue, we should be continually making nearer and nearer approaches to the most perfect and the most happy being. By this conduct, we, as the scriptures assure us, should be made partakers of the "divine nature, be born of God, and be perfect as our heavenly father is perfect." And can that be without being as happy as we are perfect? Hence, we may contemplate the great dignity of our rational nature, since our reason for kind, though not for degree, is of the same nature with that of God's. Nay, it is our reason which makes us the image of God himself and is the common bond which unites heaven and Earth, the creatures and the creator. And if our happiness is limited, it is because our reason is so. It is God alone who has an unlimited reason and happiness.

The excellent author just now mentioned [Dr. John Scott] says, "The best thing we can receive from God is himself, and himself we do receive in our strict compliance with the eternal laws of goodness. Which laws being transcribed from the nature of God, from his eternal righteousness and goodness, we do, by obeying them, derive God's nature into our own. So that while we write after the copy of his laws, we write out the perfections of his being. And his laws being the seal on which he has engraved his nature, we, in obeying them, take impression from them and stamp his blessed nature on our own."

# Appendix

## *A Catalogue of the Jesus-centered Deists*

**John Adams** (1735-1826) was the second president of the United States. He thought that Christianity was a divine revelation but that the Bible was very inaccurate and corrupt in many places. A good introduction to his Jesus-centered deism is two letters he wrote to Thomas Jefferson, one written on November 4, 1816 and the other written on November 14, 1813. It is also helpful to read the letter he wrote to F. A. van der Kemp on December 27, 1816.

**Thomas Amory** (1691?-1788?) was an English writer whose popular novels were full of theological discussions. He accepted the whole Bible, thought Jesus was a divine being, but also praised the deists and called himself a *Christian deist*. The best way to understand his Jesus-centered deism is reading *The Memoirs of Several Ladies of Great Britain* (London, 1755), 213-4, 513-27, 269-82.

**Peter Annet** (1693-1769) was an English schoolmaster who was fired after he ridiculed Christianity. He rejected the Old Testament and thought true Christianity was the same as deism. For an introduction to his Jesus-centered deism read *A Collection of the Tracts of a Certain Free Enquirer, Noted by his Sufferings for his Opinions* (London, 1739), 120-50.

**Anonymous** (fl. 1740s) wrote *The Reformation Reformed: Or, An Attempt Towards Uniting all Protestants in One Opinion Concerning Religion and Government* (London, 1743). He said the Old Testament had nothing to do with "true Christianity." A good summary of his Jesus-centered deism is pages 43-60 of this book.

**Anonymous** (fl. 1750s) wrote *A Dissertation Proving the Light of the Gospel is the Light of Nature* (London, 1756). He believed Jesus' teachings were about every person's inner Christ. A good summary of his Jesus-centered deism can be found in pages iii-viii & 1-32 of this book.

**Anonymous** (fl. 1754) wrote the pamphlet *Beweis eines Materialisten: von der Wahrheit der Christlichen Religion* (Berlin, 1754). He accepted Jesus' teachings as reported in the Bible but rejected many traditional Christian teachings. Pages 9-30 of this pamphlet are a good introduction to his Jesus-centered deism.

**Anonymous** (fl. 1789) wrote the pamphlet *Glaubensbekenntniß eines Deisten in einem vertrauten Briefe an* * [sic] (Berlin, 1789). He thought Jesus' moral teachings were the best of any person in history, but the anonymous author did not think Jesus worked any miracles. A good summary of his Jesus-centered deism is pages 9-35 of this pamphlet.

**Anonymous** (fl. 1790s) was the author of the short pamphlet *Des pretres et des cultes* (Paris, 179?). He believed Jesus taught only the simple moral message of deism.

**Walter Awberry** (fl. 1731) wrote the essay "To the Publisher of the Independent Whig." In this essay, he praised the Jesus-centered deism that had been advocated in *The Independent Whig*. Awberry's essay is printed in Thomas Gordon, *The Independent Whig*, 8th ed., 4 vols. (London, 1733), 1:xxxv-lxxii. ("W. A." is identified as Walter Awberry in the *Dictionary of National Biography*, ed. Sidney Lee, vol. 62 (New York: The Macmillan Company, 1900), 140.

**Carl Friedrich Bahrdt** (1741-1792) was Germany's most notorious deist. He revered Jesus and often prayed but thought Jesus was a member of a secret society that helped him fake his miracles. The best introduction to his deist ideas is his *Die sämtlichen Reden Jesu . . . Jesu*, vol. 2 (Berlin, 1787), iii-36.

**François Nicolas Bénoist-Lamothe** (fl. 1797) was the French rector of a school in Sens. He combined the deist religion of Theophilanthropy with some of the practices of Catholicism. The best introduction to his deist ideas is his short pamphlet *Discours sur la religion naturelle et sur le culte de la raison, prononcé dans le Temple de la Raison à Sens*, le 10 Floréal (Sens, 1794).

**Thomas Bewick** (1753-1828) was a celebrated English wood engraver who specialized in very small engravings. He believed Jesus' real teachings were deism. A very good summary of his Jesus-centered deism is *A Memoir of Thomas Bewick: Written by Himself*, ed. Iain Bain (London: Oxford University Press, 1975), 211-26.

**Franz Theodor Biergans** (1768-1847) was a former priest who became a French Revolutionary and wrote the periodical *Brutus*. He thought Jesus was the most eminent of the philosophers. Biergans also maintained that Jesus taught only the

*Appendix*

moral principles of natural religion and that the Old Testament had no relationship with genuine Christianity. The best introduction to his deist ideas is *Brutus oder Der Tyrannenfeind*, vol. 1 (n. p., 1793-4), 142-7, 101-2, 135-6, 229-238.

**Abraham Binns** (fl. 1790s) was an English writer who believed the only true parts of the Bible were the parts that were compatible with morality and science. He expressed his ideas in his short pamphlet *Remarks on a Publication, Entitled, "A Serious Admonition to the Disciples of Thomas Paine, and all Other Infidels"* (Stockport, 1796).

**Lord Bolingbroke**, aka Henry St. John, (1678-1751) was a leader of the conservative Tory party in England when he was young. However, he supported the Jacobite rebellion against George I and had to go into exile for a while. He revered Jesus and the pure Christianity Jesus taught, but he believed Jesus' teachings had been perverted by Platonic ideas blended into Christianity by theologians. One introduction to his Jesus-centered deism is *The Philosophical Works of the Late Right Honorable Henry St. John, Lord Viscount Bolingbroke* (London, 1754), 5:361-79.

**Alexander Campbell** (fl. 1750) was a former sailor who survived the mutiny of the crew of the HMS Wager. According to Campbell, true Christianity had nothing to do with the Old Testament. His only book was *An Examination of Lord Bolingbroke's Letters on History*, 2nd ed. (London, 1753), and pages 1-33 are a good introduction to his ideas.

**Thomas Chubb** (1679-1747) grew up in a very poor English family and worked in a candle shop. He revered Jesus' original teachings but did not revere the Bible as he thought it was an inaccurate account of Jesus' teachings. A good way to understand his deism is reading *The Posthumous Works of Thomas Chubb*, vol. 2 (London, 1748), 1-50.

**Anthony Collins** (1676-1729) was an English country squire whose Jesus-centered deism was influenced by radical continental ideas. A decent summary of his religious ideas is his *A Discourse of Free-Thinking* (London, 1713), 1-41.

**Christian Tobias Damm** (1699-1778) was the German rector of the well-known Köllnische Gymnasium in Berlin as well as being a celebrated Greek scholar. He thought the Bible was the best collection of godly writings, but it, especially the Old Testament, was far from an accurate account of God's activities in the world. The best introduction to his deist ideas is his book *Betrachtungen über die Religion*, Part 3-4 (Berlin, 1773), 153-169.

**Denis Driscol** (1762-1811) was the Irish editor of the American deist periodical *The Temple of Reason*. The best introduction to his Jesus-centered deism is the *The Temple of Reason*, 15 November 1800, 2-5, & 22 November 1800, 1-4.

**Daniel Isaac Eaton** (1753-1814) was a printer who published many radical periodicals and books. He claimed to be a Christian but thought the Old Testament had nothing to do with Christianity. The best way to understand his Jesus-centered deism is reading *The Trial of Mr. Daniel Isaac Eaton for Publishing the Third and Last Part of Paine's Age of Reason* (London, 1812), 23-60.

**Johann Christian Edelmann** (1698-1767) was a German writer who closely studied the ideas of Spinoza. A good introduction to Edelmann's religious ideas is Henning Graf Reventlow, *History of Biblical Interpretation*, vol. 4, trans. Leo G. Perdue (Atlanta: Society of Biblical Literature, 2010), 144-55.

**Thomas Edwards** (d. 1810) was an editor and minister at Cambridge University. He said anyone who believed in Jesus' Resurrection was a Christian, and he also thought there were many errors in the Bible. The best way to understand his Jesus-centered deism is reading his short pamphlet *A Discourse on the Limits and Importance of Free Enquiry in Matters of Religion* (Bury, 1792).

**Etignard** (fl. 1793) was a former French priest who expressed his deist ideas in a speech he gave December 10, 1793 at the Temple of Reason in France. He thought the deistic moral message of Jesus and the apostles was perverted by the Catholic popes. His speech is printed in the *Archives parlementaires de 1787 à 1860* (Paris: Centre National de la Recherche Scientifique, 1962): series 1, vol. 84, 143-5.

**Abel Fornand-Bauvinay** (1751-1824) was a French lawyer, journalist, and administrator. He thought Jesus was the wisest and most moral of all men. He also believed that Jesus taught the same natural religion that Numa, Confucius, Moses and Muhammad had taught. The best introduction to his deist ideas is his pamphlet *Religion naturelle: quelles sont les institutions religieuses qui peuvent contribuer à propager les vertus d'un peuple libre* (Paris, 1798), 7-21 & 28-35.

**Ben Franklin** (1706-1790) was one of the eighteenth-century's greatest scientists as well as the American ambassador to France during the Revolutionary War. He identified true Christianity with Jesus' teachings and rejected any Christian teaching, such as original sin, that portrayed God as less than totally good and fair. A good introduction to his early Jesus-centered deism is his short pamphlet *A Defence of the Rev. Mr. Hemphill's Observations: Or, an Answer to the Vindication of the Reverend Commission* (Philadelphia, 1735). The best introduction to his later ideas is his March 9, 1790 letter to Ezra Stiles.

**Johannes Frey** (1743-1800) was a Swiss schoolteacher and active supporter of the Helvetic Republic. He was disciplined several times by the school authorities for teaching unconventional and unorthodox ideas about Christianity. The best introduction to his deist ideas is his *Eine Predigt über die Aufklärung* (Basel?, 1789), 3-10.

**Friend to Truth** (fl. 1780s) wrote *Observations Upon the Four Gospels Shewing Their Defects... By Authority* (Geneva, 1789). He agreed Jesus worked miracles but thought

*Appendix*

the Bible was too inconsistent to be an accurate report of Jesus' life. A quick summary of his Jesus-centered deism is pages 337-50 of this book.

**Pierre Gallet** (17??-18??) was a French writer. He thought true Christianity was the simple morality that Jesus taught. Gallet also believed that Jesus taught purer moral doctrines than other religious teachers, such as Zoroaster or Confucius. A good introduction to his deist ideas is *Le véritable évangile, par le citoyen Gallet*, 2nd ed. (Paris, 1793/4), i-xvi.

**Léonard Gay-Vernon** (1748-1822) was a French priest who was elected bishop of the Constitutional Church during the French Revolution. He was also elected a deputy to the National Convention and a member of the Council of Five Hundred. He thought original Christianity was simple morality, but the Catholic popes had corrupted it. The best introduction to his deist ideas is his letter in the *Journal du département de la Haute-Vienne*, 14 November 1793, 93-5, and his *Lettre Pastorale* (n. p., 1793), 1-4, 10-11.

**Henri François Godineau** (fl. 1793) was a former French priest who gave a speech at the National Club of Bordeaux in 1793. Godineau believed Jesus taught a simple message of loving God and one's neighbors, but his disciples and later followers mixed many extraneous elements into this simple message. Goudineau's speech is reprinted in the *Temple of Reason*, 16 September 1801, 286-7.

**Thomas Gordon** (c. 1691-1750) was the Scottish writer of many essays that were very widely read in colonial America. He claimed to revere the whole Bible but did not accept many traditional Christian teachings. The best way to understand his Jesus-centered deism is reading the essay "In what only True Religion Consists" in the *Independent Whig* (London, 1721), 429-44.

**James Edward Hamilton** (fl. 1790s) claimed to share the beliefs of the earliest Christians. The best way to understand his deism is reading the ending section labelled "To the Reader" in his book *Strictures upon Primitive Christianity . . . Mr. Babcock: Part the Second* (London, 1792), 1-12.

**John Henley** (1692-1756), a former minister in the Church of England, was extremely well-known for his performances at his church/school called the Oratory. He believed Jesus' true teachings had been misinterpreted, and he advocated a mystical interpretation of these teachings. A good summary of his Jesus-centered deism is his very short book *The Coup de Grace: or, Mr. Bayle's Prophecy Fulfilled*, 4th ed. (London, 1745).

**John Holwell** (1711-1798) worked in India as a surgeon until he eventually was appointed to various offices for the East India Company. He claimed the angelic being that was Jesus also taught the same principles in India when this being made a divine revelation there. The best way to understand his Jesus-centered deism is reading *Interesting Historical Events, Relative to the Provinces of Bengal... Part III* (London, 1771), 41-91.

**Thomas Jefferson** (1743-1826) wrote the *Declaration of Independence* and was the third president of the United States. He revered Jesus but did not believe in miracles or that the Old Testament was part of true Christianity. A good introduction to his deist ideas are his letters to William Short (Aug 4, 1820), to Dr. Benjamin Waterhouse (June 26, 1822), and to Dr. Benjamin Rush (April 21, 1803).

**Soame Jenyns** (1704-1787) was a very well-known English politician and writer. He believed Jesus' moral teachings were so pure that they had to be a divine revelation, but he also believed in reincarnation. A summary of his Jesus-centered deism is in *A View of the Internal Evidence of the Christian Religion*, 3rd ed. (London, 1776), 115-33.

**Julius Friedrich Knüppeln** (1757-1840) was a German editor and writer. He thought Christianity was the best religion but rejected the Old Testament. A good introduction to his deist ideas is his *Philosophische Skizze von Berlin*, vol. 1 (Leipzig, 1788), 156-76.

**Francis Lodwick** (1619-94) belonged to the Royal Society as well as being a merchant. He never published his religious manuscripts, but they were published recently in *On Language, Theology and Utopia*, edited by Felicity Henderson and William Poole (Oxford: Clarendon Press, 2011). Lodwick thought Jesus had been sent by God to recall people to the truths of natural religion. A good summary of his Jesus-centered deism can be found on pages 171-99, 209-15, 243-5, & 270-8 of this book.

**M. E.** (fl. 1794) was an unknown author who wrote about religion and God during the French Revolution for the newspaper Argos. He thought Jesus' original teachings were the same as the principles behind the French Revolution. The best introduction to his ideas is *Argos, oder der Mann mit hundert Augen* [Argos, or the Man with a Hundred Eyes], ed. J. F. Butenschön, vol. 4 (n. p., 1794), 365-7, 499-506, 531-4, 303-4, & 257-60.

**Conyers Middleton** (1683-1750) was an English Doctor of Divinity who was in charge of Cambridge University's library. He believed true Christianity could be intellectually defended but only if some traditional theological positions were abandoned. A good summary of his Jesus-centered deism is *The Miscellaneous Works of the Late Reverend and Learned Conyers Middleton* (London, 1752), 2:144-51 & 304-16.

**Misophenax** (fl. 1762) was an anonymous person who wrote *Christianity True Deism* (London, 1762). He thought true Christianity was the same as deism, but he also thought Jesus was more than a mere human and the Hebrew prophets had been divinely inspired. The best way to understand his Jesus-centered deism is to read 35-81 in this book.

**Thomas Morgan** (1671/2-1743) was a Welsh writer who lost his position as a Presbyterian minister because of his unorthodox ideas. He labelled himself a *Christian* *deist* and thought that there was no relationship between genuine Christianity and the Old Testament. A good summary of his Jesus-centered deism is *The Moral Philosopher*, 2nd ed., vol. 1 (London, 1738), iii-xii, 142-70.

**Andreas Moser** (1766-1806) was a German school teacher and writer. The best expression of his deist ideas is his *Gesunder Menschenverstand über die Kunst Völker zu beglücken*, 2nd ed. (n. p., 1807), 48-73.

**Jean-Baptiste Mosneron de Launay** (1738-1830) was a French writer of tragedies as well as being politically active during the French Revolution. He thought Jesus was the greatest of men, but Mosneron did not think Jesus had ever worked any miracles. The best introduction to his deist ideas is his book *Vie du législateur des Chrétiens, sans lacunes et sans miracles* (Paris, 1803), 18-38.

**L.- L. Pélissard** (fl. 1798) was a French writer. He thought Jesus was the greatest of philosophers and was the greatest practitioner of the deist religion of Theophilanthropy. A good introduction to his deist ideas is pages 1-14 of his pamphlet *L'origine du culte romain et de la théophilantropie; avec une dissertation sur l'Apocalypse de saint Jean, qui a prédit tous les évenemens actuels* (Paris, 1798).

**James Pitt** (fl. 1714-1755) was the English editor for the *London Journal* in the late 1720s and early 1730s. He also wrote articles in this journal using the pen names of "Socrates" and "Publicola." He believed genuine Christianity was the same as the original moral teachings of Jesus. A good summary of his Jesus-centered deism is two articles in the *London Journal*: "An Essay on Original Primitive Christianity," published on November 15, 1729, and "The Vindication of Lord Shaftesbury's Writings, Continued," published on June 17, 1732.

**Rational Christian** (fl. 1760s) wrote *The Morality of the New Testament Digested Under Various Heads* (London, 1765). He thought true Christianity was taught merely in the Gospels, and they only taught the basic principles of deism. A good summary of his Jesus-centered deism is in pages 1-39 and 58-70 of this book.

**Andreas Riem** (1749-1814) was a German preacher for a number of years before he worked as an editor, writer, and publisher. He said that Jesus' pure teachings were the best religion ever. He also rejected the whole Old Testament and thought that both Moses and Jesus never did any miracles. The best introduction to his Jesus-centered deism is *Das reinere Christenthum oder die Religion der Kinder des Lichts* (Berlin, 1789), 1-33.

**Friedrich Heinrich Emil Schnaar** (1755-1833) was a German editor and professor of philosophy at Rinteln, Germany. Schnaar thought nature was the only revelation God ever made and Jesus was the master interpreter of nature. The best introduction to his deist ideas is his article, "Was ist Natur, Bibel und Jesus?" *Der Genius der Zeit* 1 (Jan-April 1794): 267-7.

**Johann Heinrich Schulz** (1739-1823) was a Lutheran minister who lost his position because he embraced deist ideas. The best introduction to his deist ideas is *Philosophische Betrachtung über Theologie und Religion . . . insonderheit*, 2nd ed. (Frankfurt, 1786), 65-89, & 163-7.

**Karl Franz Schwind** (1764-1848) was a former Catholic priest and professor of theology at the University at Strasburg. He thought the Old Testament presented a childish view of God, but he believed Jesus was born of a virgin. The best introduction to his deist ideas is the first 20 pages of his book *Ueber die ältesten heiligen Semitischen Denkmäler: Eine Abhandlung unsrer [sic] theologischen Routine entgegen* (Strasburg, 1792).

**T.** (fl. 1793) was the anonymous author of a short essay in Franz Theodor Biergans' periodical *Brutus oder Der Tyrannenfeind*, vol. 2 (n. p., 1793-4), 81-92. In this short essay, T. denigrated priestly religion and said Jesus taught only simple virtues.

**Matthew Tindal** (1657-1733) was an Oxford University fellow and a lawyer. He thought real Christianity was the same as natural religion. A very good summary of his Jesus-centered deism is in *Christianity as Old as the Creation: Or, the Gospel a Republication of the Religion of Nature* (London, 1731), 1-54.

**John Toland** (1670-1722) was an Irish editor and writer who eventually accepted pantheism. A good introduction to his deist ideas is his *A Collection of Several Pieces of Mr. John Toland*, vol. 2 (London, 1726), 130-9.

**John Trenchard** (1662-1723) was an English writer and lawyer whose essays were widely read by colonial Americans. He believed the Bible was divinely inspired, but he thought priests and ministers had added many false doctrines to true Christianity. The best summary of his Jesus-centered deism is the essay "In what only True Religion Consists" on pages 429-44 of the *Independent Whig* (London, 1721).

www.ingramcontent.com/pod-product-compliance
Lightning Source LLC
Chambersburg PA
CBHW040233110526
44582CB00002B/43